Handley Carr G. Moule

**Colossian Studies**

lessons in faith and holiness from St. Paul's Epistles to the Colossians and Philemon

Handley Carr G. Moule
**Colossian Studies**
*lessons in faith and holiness from St. Paul's Epistles to the Colossians and Philemon*
ISBN/EAN: 9783337381349

Printed in Europe, USA, Canada, Australia, Japan

Cover: Foto ©Lupo / pixelio.de

More available books at **www.hansebooks.com**

# COLOSSIAN STUDIES

LESSONS IN FAITH AND HOLINESS
FROM ST PAUL'S EPISTLES TO THE COLOSSIANS
AND PHILEMON

H. C. G. MOULE, D.D.

PRINCIPAL OF RIDLEY HALL, AND FORMERLY FELLOW OF TRINITY
COLLEGE, CAMBRIDGE

NEW YORK
A. C. ARMSTRONG AND SON
51, EAST TENTH STREET
1898

TO THE

# RIGHT REVEREND JOHN CHARLES RYLE, D.D.

### BISHOP OF LIVERPOOL

THIS BOOK IS INSCRIBED

WITH REVERENT AND GRATEFUL AFFECTION

BY HIS SERVANT AND FRIEND

> Our glorious Leader claims our praise
> For His own pattern given,
> And the long cloud of witnesses
> Shew the same path to heaven.
> WATTS

# PREFACE

THE "Studies" now in the reader's hand have been written with the single object of assisting and stimulating those other "studies" which the Christian can and must carry on by himself alone, with his own Bible before him.

It will soon be found out how different is the purpose of these pages from that of the complete and elaborated critical commentary. In one respect only shall I seem to have traversed the lines of that sort of exposition—in the attempt to render every word of the text with careful regard to diction and connexion. I have sought to take the Apostle's sentences up, one by one, as if they met my eye for the first time (in a certain respect), and to turn them into English so as to convey the freshness of the impression.

When this has been accomplished, with whatever measure of success, my sole further purpose has been to bring out for the reader's notice some of those inexhaustible messages for the soul which the study of the God-given utterances of the Apostle has carried home to myself.

May the heavenly Master, the same yesterday, and to-day, and for ever, be pleased to make some use of His servant's unworthy labours, to the benefit of His Church, in the unending and delightful work of "reading, marking, and inwardly digesting" the Word of peace, of hope, of holiness, of heaven.

    RIDLEY HALL, CAMBRIDGE.
        *March*, 1898.

# CONTENTS

## THE EPISTLE TO THE COLOSSIANS

### CHAPTER I

|  | PAGE |
|---|---|
| INTRODUCTORY . . . . . . | 3 |

### CHAPTER II

SALUTATION AND THANKSGIVING: NEWS OF CHRISTIAN
LIFE AT COLOSSÆ . . . . . . 25
(COLOSSIANS i. 1–8.)

### CHAPTER III

THE APOSTLE'S PRAYER FOR THE COLOSSIANS . . 47
(COLOSSIANS i. 9–14.)

### CHAPTER IV

THE PRE-EMINENCE OF THE SON OF GOD . 71
(COLOSSIANS i. 15–20.)

## CHAPTER V

REDEMPTION APPLIED: THE CASE OF THE COLOSSIANS: THE APOSTLE'S JOY AND AIM . . 93
(COLOSSIANS i. 21–29.)

## CHAPTER VI

THE SECRET OF GOD, AND ITS POWER . 117
(COLOSSIANS ii. 1–7.)

## CHAPTER VII

PARDON, LIFE, AND VICTORY IN THE CRUCIFIED AND RISEN ONE . . . 139
(COLOSSIANS ii. 8–15.)

## CHAPTER VIII

HOLY LIBERTY IN UNION WITH CHRIST . 163
(COLOSSIANS ii. 16–23.)

## CHAPTER IX

THE ROOT AND FRUIT OF HOLINESS . . 187
(COLOSSIANS iii. 1–7.)

## CHAPTER X

MORE UPON HOLINESS, ITS RULES AND MOTIVES  209
(COLOSSIANS iii. 8–17.)

## CHAPTER XI

THE CHRISTIAN HOME . 231
(COLOSSIANS iii. 18—iv. 1.)

## CHAPTER XII

LAST WORDS ON PRAYER, CONDUCT, SPEECH: PERSONAL MESSAGES: FAREWELL . 255
(COLOSSIANS iv. 2–18.)

# THE EPISTLE TO PHILEMON

## CHAPTER XIII

THE EPISTLE TO PHILEMON: INTRODUCTORY . 279

## CHAPTER XIV

THE EPISTLE TO PHILEMON: TRANSLATION: *ENVO* . 303

WELL does the Lord call the Scriptures *the Door*. For the Scriptures bring us to God, and open to us the knowledge of Him. The Scriptures make the sheep, and guard the sheep, and do not suffer the wolf to enter in.—ST CHRYSOSTOM, *on John* x.

*INTRODUCTORY*

When quiet in my house I sit
   Thy Book is my companion still;
My joy Thy sayings to repeat,
   Talk o'er the records of Thy will,
And search the oracles divine
Till every heart-felt word be mine.

Oh may the gracious words divine
   Subject of all my converse be;
So will the Lord His follower join
   And walk and talk Himself with me;
So shall my heart His presence prove,
And burn with everlasting love.

C. Wesley.

# CHAPTER I

## INTRODUCTORY

THE purpose of the following pages is altogether devotional. To speak more exactly, my aim is to assist the believing reader of the Epistle to the Colossians not in the way of historical and critical discussion (for which the Epistle offers rich material) but in the way of such exposition and reflection as may, under the blessing of God, tend to edify. Throughout the expository portions will run a careful translation, and it will be necessary in the course of this to remark upon words and grammar. Inevitably also there will come in references to history and to geography. Yet for a treatment of many topics prominent in the strict critical discussion of Colossians the reader will look here in vain; they will not be touched upon, or at most the allusion will be passing.

For example, I avoid altogether the much agitated problem of St Paul's route on his third missionary journey. That problem involves the question whether St Paul, on his way through the "inner regions" of Asia Minor to Ephesus (Acts xix. 1), when he "went over all the Phrygian and Galatian country" (xviii. 23), did or did not pass down the river-valley in which Colossæ stood. This question has of course its interest, as every detail in that wonderful life has. But it does not materially affect the sort of study of the Epistle which I have in view; for on any theory St Paul had never *stayed* at Colossæ when he wrote the Epistle to the Colossians. If he did pass there, it was at most but "as a wayfaring man that turneth aside to tarry for a night." When he wrote, the Colossian mission-converts, as a body, had "not seen his face in the flesh" (ii. 1).

Nor shall I discuss at any length the question whether or no the Epistle was written not from Rome but from Cæsarea on the Sea, where (Acts xxiv. 27) St Paul spent two years in forced retirement. The question has been elaborately debated in modern times; and no one who has not studied it should lightly think that the case for Rome is self-evident. For myself, the conviction is complete that Rome *was* the place of the writing of the Epistle.[1] And this position will be assumed throughout the exposition. But for our purpose this also is a question of no primary importance. The allusions to the Writer's position and condition in the Epistle are very slight indeed; a contrast to the graphic touches of Philippians. We hear of a "fellow-prisoner" (iv. 10), and of "sufferings" in which the Apostle "rejoices" (i. 24), and of brethren, few among many, who are "a comfort" to him (iv. 11). And in the companion Letter, or rather Note, to Philemon, we have repeated allusions to a captivity (1, 9, 10, 13). But these references could hardly be made

---

[1] In *The Cambridge Bible for Schools, etc.* (*Colossians*, Introduction, ch. ii.), I have attempted to state carefully the evidence on the two sides.

more significant for our purpose by any discovery for certain that Rome or that Cæsarea was the place where the Writer was detained.

Again, the relation in time between Philippians and this Epistle will not be discussed. It will be enough for me, meaning what I do in this exposition, to refer thus once and briefly to it, for it has little bearing, if any, on the positive revelations and messages of Colossians. I am then one of (I admit) the few who go altogether in this matter with the reasonings and conclusions of Lightfoot in his commentary on Philippians. I am convinced, after all I have read to the contrary, that Philippians comes early in St Paul's Roman imprisonment, and that Colossians (with Ephesians and Philemon) comes later. I would date Philippians A.D. 61, and Colossians perhaps as late as the spring of A.D. 63.[1] This will be assumed in the following pages. But I think it will

---

[1] See *The Cambridge Bible*, etc. (*Colossians*, Introduction, ch. ii., and *Philippians*, Introd., ch. ii.), for a statement of the questions involved.

be seen that such an assumption will leave the study of the divine message of Colossians very much alone. It may here and there give to our picture of the Apostle as he writes a colour which the reader may think borrowed too freely from imagination. But if so, he will easily obliterate it in his mind; and what the Apostle has actually written will remain as it stands, in its truth and glory.

Another question presented by the Epistle calls for ample discussion from the critical expounder, but may be stated with much more brevity for our purpose. I mean the question, what was the special form of religious error which had invaded the Colossian Mission, when Epaphras came to St Paul to report upon the state of things, and especially upon a dangerous propaganda which was unsettling the converts. Certain features of this mischief are apparent at first sight, and are recognized by all students of the Epistle. It was evidently in some sort and degree Judaistic. It insisted upon circumcision, and upon the observance of the Jewish holy days, weekly, monthly, and yearly (ii. 16). It laid a strong emphasis upon "ordinances" of restriction in food and drink. The difficult question in the case is how far these elements do or do not explain *the whole* movement. Was it, or was it not, simply the Judæo-Christianity which had withstood St Paul at Antioch (Acts xv.), and later in Galatia? Was it this and no more, or was it this affected and altered by more mystic elements from "the pensive East"; by speculations on the mysteries of Being, and of Evil?[1] In other words, was "the Colossian Heresy" an amalgam of Judaism and Gnosticism, in a wide reference of the latter word? My belief is that on the whole this view of the matter is the right one, and that this alone fully satisfies the language of some parts of the Epistle. But it will be best to consider the question as it comes up from time to time in the text itself. And it must be considered with a caution emphasized by the fact that in our English expository literature the great

---

[1] See Mansel's *Gnostic Heresies*, Lecture i., for an able statement of the constant presence to the Gnostic of the two great enigmas, the Origin of finite Being, and of Evil.

names of Lightfoot and Hort appear in it on opposite sides.

One thing is certain as to "the Colossian Heresy." It was a doctrine of God, and of salvation, which cast a cloud over the glory of Jesus Christ. For the present at least, it will be enough to remember this. St Paul, writing to Colossæ, had to deal with an error which, whatever else it did, did this—it put Jesus Christ into the background. It found the Pauline converts, we may safely assume, acting upon the Pauline Gospel; "worshipping by God's Spirit, exulting in Christ Jesus, and confident—but not in the flesh" (Phil. iii. 3). They had heard a message which was, first and last, JESUS CHRIST—"who died for our sins, and rose again for our justification," and lives to be our life, by His all-sufficient grace. Their baptism had been to them the divine seal and summary of all this; and in the strong simplicity of first faith and love they were enjoying "the light of the Lord," without a misgiving. But then came in certain messengers who undertook to set them right; to shew them what they did not fully understand.

Jesus Christ might be much, but He was not all. The Law was still the fence around the Gospel. Baptism must be approached through circumcision, or at least supported by it. The believer must be a devotee, in an ordered round of qualifying observances; or he would not be acceptable, or pure. And while Jesus Christ, in the vast hierarchy of the Unseen, occupied no doubt a place of majesty, He must not cast into the shade other powers of that world. The disciple must know that the Angels of glory called also for his worship, and for his reliance. They, with the Christ, as the Christ with them, were necessary links in the mysterious chain which must put man on earth, man in the body, man in matter, in contact with the Eternal. Would they have rest to their consciences? They must supplement Christ with other mediations. Would they have emancipation from evil and its tyranny? They must supplement Christ with a strict ascetic and ritual discipline.

It is perfectly clear that the new propagandists did not, at least in any avowed and perhaps in any intentional way, deny Jesus

Christ as the Leader and in some sense the Saviour and Lord of men. There is no hint in the Epistle that the Colossians had ever heard His blessed Name blasphemed by their visitors; as it would have been by emissaries of a Caiaphas, or again by accomplices of a Demetrius the silversmith. Probably the new Gospel was very far indeed from confessing anything like the true glory of Christ's Person; He probably was, in it, by no means "the Son of God with power." Yet He was enough acknowledged to allow the teachers to pass, even in their own eyes, for "brethren." Only, there was this fatal difference; He was practically minimized. He might in some sense preside over the difficult processes of religion. But He was not—Salvation. He was something. He was some great thing. But He was very far indeed from All. He was mysterious and venerable. But He was not "the Way, and the Truth, and the Life"; "Righteousness, and Sanctification, and Redemption"; Light and Love, and Power; "Alpha and Omega." The new voices at Colossæ would have many things to discourse upon; and among those many things would be Jesus Christ. But He would not be the magnetic Centre of their discourses. They would not gravitate to Him, and be as if they could never have done with setting forth His holy greatness, and His vital necessity, and His "all-sufficiency in all things." His dying love would not set the speakers' hearts and words on fire, nor would they dilate upon His rising power, and the double blessedness of His presence, for His disciples upon the Throne, and in His disciples in the heart. The wonder of His Incarnation would be little spoken of, and the solemn joy of the hope of His Return as little. The favourite topics of conversation and of preaching would be of a very different kind. Circumcision, a calendar of obligatory holidays, a code of ceremonial abstinence, a philosophy of unseen powers, and secret ways and rules for approach to them in adoration; these would be the congenial and really characteristic themes of this "other Gospel."

Now this, as we know, (thanks under God to our Colossian Epistle among other oracles of the Truth,) is exactly *un*like the authentic

Gospel. What is the Gospel of the New Testament, or rather of the whole Scriptures, as the New Testament unfolds the hidden glories of the Old? It is not this thing, or that, and the other; it is our Lord Jesus Christ. It is "the proclamation of Jesus Christ." He is, in it, "the First, and with the last." From every point of view it is thus in the Gospel. Do we approach the Gospel to ask for oracles about God? It replies that Jesus Christ is "the express Image of His Person," One with Him. Do we come to ask answers about the mystery of Being, the majestic secret of Creation? It replies that "all things were made through the Son, and without Him was not anything made that was made." Do we interrogate the Gospel about pardon? Its answer, full of the musical harmony of eternal Law and eternal Love, tells us that "the blood of Jesus Christ His Son cleanseth us from all sin"; that we are "accepted in the Beloved"; that our "sins are forgiven us for His Name's sake"; for "He is the Propitiation for our sins." Do we enquire about the inmost way of Holiness? We listen, and learn that "if the Son shall make us free, we shall be free indeed"; "He is made unto us Sanctification"; He is able to "dwell in our hearts, by faith," and thence to rule our being; "His grace is sufficient"; "His power overshadows" us in our deep moral weakness. Do we feel the burthen of our awful mortality, and ask for a real antidote? He Himself answers, out of the heart of His Gospel, "I am the Resurrection and the Life"; "He that believeth in Me hath everlasting life"; "shall never die." His servant says that "He hath abolished death," and that He, the blessed Lord of Resurrection, "is able to subdue all things unto Himself." Do we come to the Gospel for an answer which shall make tangible to us the infinite mystery of the future life? "To depart and to be with Christ is far better"; that is the answer for death. "We shall be for ever with the Lord"; that is the answer for resurrection.

Yes indeed, in the Gospel of God, of Christ, of the Apostles, of the Prophets, Christ is ALL. He is the Revelation of the Father, the Bond of Man and God, the Giver of the Spirit, the Merit of the guilty, the Purity of the sinful, the Power of the weak, the everlasting Life for our mortality.

No surer test, according to the Holy Scriptures, can be applied to anything claiming to be Christian teaching, than this: Where does it put Jesus Christ? What does it make of Jesus Christ? Is He something in it, or is He all? Is He the Sun of the true solar system, so that every planet gets its place and its light from Him? Or is He at best a sort of Ptolemaic sun, rolling together with other luminaries around an earthly centre—whether that centre take the form of an observance, a constitution, or a philosophy?

If such is the character of the one Gospel which has really descended from the heavens, it is no wonder that St Paul takes the line he does in writing to Colossæ. From first to last the dogmatics of the Epistle consist in just this, the infinite glory of the Person of the Son of God, and the grandeur of His finished Work, and the abundant fulness of His Grace. And the noble ethics of the Epistle are just this, the Son of God applied to the believer's daily path, in this perfection of what He is and what He has done. We shall appreciate this better of course as we proceed. But let it guide and govern our studies from the beginning, as it is so amply entitled to do. We are to read an inspired Epistle, an Oracle of God, whose utterances are conditioned by the approach of a theory of religion which puts Jesus Christ out of the central place. Let us listen to the sentences and paragraphs; they will more than re-affirm all the oracles that have gone before concerning this wonderful Saviour. They will assert again and again eternal truths which earlier Scriptures have emphasized. But they will lift the veil still further from His inexhaustible glory, as they tell us things about which we had not so explicitly heard before—about His Headship in Creation, and His Headship in the Church; about His being our very Life; "that in all things He may have the pre-eminence."

So be it, with us now, as in Colossæ then.

And where, and what, was Colossæ? It

was a country-town of Asia Minor, about a hundred miles east of Ephesus. It lay at the mouth of "a narrow glen some ten miles long,"[1] on the south of which towers Mount Cadmus, a snowy pyramid, now called by the Turks Baba Dagh, Father of Mountains. Down the glen, and out of it, runs the Lycus, the Wolf-stream, soon to pour its waters into the Mæander. Within the day's walk of an active pedestrian, in the same Lycus valley, lie the sites of Laodicea and of Hierapolis, looking at each other across the fields and the river. It is a strange region, betraying everywhere the presence of volcanic fires, and the traces of their action; an action which has repeatedly in the past devastated the district, and which struck Colossæ itself with ruinous shocks within a few years after the writing of the Epistle.[2] Travellers describe with equal warmth the splendid picturesqueness of the scenery, seen under the glowing sun of Asia, and the weird desolateness of the streams

---

[1] Ramsay, *The Church in the Roman Empire*, p. 472.
[2] See Lightfoot, *Colossians*, ed. i., p. 38, note.

and cascades of limestone which whiten the sides of the valley.

Of the three towns of the Lycus, Colossæ was by far the smallest, and at the date of the Epistle it was in a state of decline and decay. It had had its days of fame. Here Xerxes had halted on his way to the Grecian wars, letting his countless host rest at the western mouth of the Cadmian pass. The younger Cyrus, the Cyrus of Xenophon's *Anabasis*, paused here for a week with his Greek mercenaries on his way upward to attack his brother; it was then "a populous and prosperous city."[1] It was celebrated too for a natural wonder; a gulph into which the Lycus disappeared, to issue five stadia lower down, before its junction with the Mæander; a limestone tunnel, which seems to have been changed long ago, by earthquake or decay, into an open cutting. But by the Christian era Colossæ was small and obscure; a place which hovered between town and village, a townlet, a *polisma*.

---

[1] Xenophon, *Anabasis*, i. 2, § 6.

We probably know, by observation or description, perhaps some of my readers by residence, what life is like in a *polisma*. It has its brighter side, of close neighbourhood and almost domestic friendships. But there is a sadder side also, a certain stagnation of thought and action, and a melancholy inseparable from what seems a destiny of decline. Let us take such impressions as a foil to the glory of the Colossian Epistle, and thank God that in that old, remote *polisma* this grace had so gloriously begun to "make all things new" in human hearts. And is it not characteristic of Him that this wonderful Epistle, this great treasure for all time in the universal Church, should have been written for *Colossæ*? It is read and pondered now wherever man has heard of Christ. It is dear to innumerable hearts in Europe, in Australia, in India, on the central table-land of Africa, in the islands of the Ocean, in the cities and on the prairies of America. But it was first sent, with all its unsearchable wealth of truth, to the mission-church of that small decaying town of the

Levant. So did the Author of Scripture "give liberally." And this liberality with His written Word long ago is an index of His heart towards the believer, and the Church, for ever. There is nothing which He will grudge, in their real need, to the feeblest of His disciples and to the least noticed of their communities.

How was Colossæ evangelized? Certainly not by the direct ministry of St Paul himself. The disciples there—as a community —"had not seen his face in the flesh." The work was probably done through the Epaphras[1] who appears so prominently in the Epistle. We may reasonably assume that Epaphras himself entered into the light of Christ as a hearer of St Paul at Ephesus, at some time during the "three whole years" (probably A.D. 55—A.D. 57) which the Apostle spent continuously in the great city. During that time "all they that dwelt in Asia," the proconsular province of which Ephesus was capital, "heard the Word" (Acts xix. 10). It

---

[1] Not to be identified with the Epaphroditus of Philippians.

was one of those periods of which the Church has seen many since, when the Spirit of God moved in human hearts with what we may presume to call an epidemic power; from town to town, from village to village, the longing to hear the heavenly message spread, men knew not how. We seem to see a group of friends coming down the Mæander valley from the quiet old town among the limestone hills; Philemon is there, and Apphia, and Archippus, and Epaphras, and perhaps Onesimus in attendance on them. And they find out the new teacher, and of some of them at least "the Lord opens the heart," and they believe on the blessed Name. And we may think that Paul soon recognizes in Epaphras the gifts of evangelist and pastor, and lays his hands on him in due time, and sends him back to be the missionary of his home.

Even thus many an incident of evangelization has been shaped in later days. There is a Colossæ-like district in the highlands of the Chinese province of Cheh-kiang, the district of Chu-ki. Not very many years ago it was evangelized by one of its own sons, who had visited Hang-chow, the Ephesus of the region, the glorious Quin-say of Marco Polo, and there had read the unknown word JESUS over the door of a mission-room. So began his enquiries, and so came his conversion, followed in time (after a period of earnest witnessing, antecedent to any ministerial calling) by his ordination as the missionary-pastor of Chu-ki.[1] The seasons and scenes are various indeed, but the power of the Gospel is above all time.

Colossæ is nothing now but ruins. Ages ago the site was deserted for Chonæ,[2] now called Chonos, three miles away. The visitor finds a field full of broken structures and mutilated columns, and at a little distance another field shewing the débris of a cemetery; the Lycus, the Tchoruk Su of the Turks, rushes as of old between. This is Colossæ.

"But the Word of the Lord endureth for ever."

---

[1] See *The Story of the Cheh-kiang Mission* (published by the Church Missionary Society), ed. 4, ch. vi.

[2] *I.e.* "the Funnels"; with allusion probably to the underground channels in the limestone.

*SALUTATION AND THANKSGIVING: NEWS OF CHRISTIAN LIFE AT COLOSSÆ*

WHAT do I not owe to the Lord for permitting me to take a part in the translation of His Word? Never did I see such wonders, and wisdom, and love, in this blessed Book as since I have been obliged to study every expression. And it is a delightful reflection that death cannot deprive us of the pleasure of studying its mysteries.

H. MARTYN.

# CHAPTER II

## SALUTATION AND THANKSGIVING: NEWS OF CHRISTIAN LIFE AT COLOSSÆ

### COLOSSIANS i. 1–8

Ver. 1. **Paul, an apostle of Christ Jesus,**[1] His commissioned Delegate to reveal, teach, and order, through God's will, the will whose sovereign efficacy makes it as it were its own *means* (διά with genitive), and **Timotheus, the brother,** the fellow-Christian and
Ver. 2. fellow-worker known to all,[2] **to the holy and faithful brethren in Christ in Colossæ,** the men and women there who, joined to the Lord, are "hallowed" from sin and the world and are living the life of "faith" in Him; **grace be to you and**

---

[1] Χριστὸς Ἰησοῦς is the best-attested order. It is almost peculiar to St Paul, and with him is the more frequent. It lays a certain emphasis on the Χριστός, and so on the Lord's Messianic glory.

[2] So I would paraphrase ὁ ἀδελφός, the words used likewise of Quartus (Rom. xvi. 23), Sosthenes (1 Cor. i. 1), Apollos (1 Cor. xvi. 12). Every Christian is an ἀδελφός among brethren (see just below, ver. 2); but ὁ ἀδελφός seems to indicate something *par excellence*.

peace, all that is free and loving in divine favour and presence, and all that is tranquil and happy in divine regard for you, and in your repose in divine salvation, **from God our Father,**[1] that Name of infinite nearness and love, revealed to us in the beloved Son, who has made us His own brethren.

Let us pause over this familiar greeting, for one simple purpose. It puts before us the persons greeted, as to their location, their connexion, from two very different points of sight. Where were these "hallowed and believing[2] brethren"? They were "*in Colossæ.*" They were "*in Christ.*" From the one side they, as much as any of their neighbours, were the denizens of that small

---

[1] Probably the words καὶ Κυρίου Ἰησοῦ Χριστοῦ in the Received Text are to be omitted; they may have been inserted early by copyists from the parallel passage Eph. i. 2. —The words just above, τοῖς ἐν Κολ. ἁγίοις καὶ πιστοῖς ἀδελφοῖς ἐν Χριστῷ, lose somewhat by translation, as it is impossible in English to keep the Greek order; "*the in Colossæ,*" etc. The change of order necessitated by our idiom throws rather too much emphasis on "in Colossæ," where emphasis should rather rest on "in Christ." And the paraphrase, "*those who in Colossæ are holy,*" etc., is not quite true to the simplicity of the Greek.

[2] N. T. usage favours our rendering πιστός here not "trusty" but "trustful." See e.g. Gal. iii. 9.

Asiatic-Greek town; probably its natives; habituated to the scenery of its streets, and fields, and rushing river, and limestone chasms, and overlooking hills, and to the scenes of its daily life in home, and shop, and market. They were "in" it, hour by hour, as to all its unfavourable spiritual circumstances; its immemorial idolatry, its pagan vice, its provincialism, its narrowness, its decay. All that was formidable in a life lived amidst old and intimate surroundings, yet with the confession of a new creed.; all that was depressing in a life lived where the stream of energy around ran low, and the "brethren" were but a little flock; this was involved in their being placed "in Colossæ." And they were as sensitive as we are to what the pressure of hour and company means for the weak human heart. But then on the other side they were, while in Colossæ, also "in Christ." Here was their supernatural secret for life, power, purity, love, cheerfulness, "everlasting comfort and good hope." Their spiritual locality was—the LORD. To Him they had "come." And so to Him, by the Spirit, they were "joined" (1 Cor. vi. 17).

And now, "with Him, in God," their life, as to its inexhaustible principle and secret, was "hid." They moved about Colossæ "in Christ." They worked, served, kept the house, followed the business, met the neighbours, entered into their sorrows and joys, "walked in wisdom towards them," suffered their abuse and insults when such things came—all "in Christ." They carried about with them a "private atmosphere," which was not of Asia but of heaven. To them Christ was the inner home, the dear invisible but real resting-place. He was "the strong City" of refuge and strength. He was the Paradise, with its deep shades, and golden flowers, and living streams. Or to put it otherwise, He was the blessed Head, "in" whom they now found themselves the limbs. "In Him" they lived and moved, as knowing that His life could indeed be trusted to fill them, and His thought and will to guide them. In Colossæ, they were yet much more in Him. And what a rich gain for poor Colossæ that they, being in Him, were in it!

As then, so now, for us who "have believed to the saving of the soul." Where are we?

In some locality of earth's surface, where the will of God has set us. Perhaps in a spot familiar to us from the dawn of memory, made to be to us what it is by a thousand associations of love, of loss, of joy, of grief; intensely near to our consciousness, whether to absorb affections or to make trial felt. Perhaps in some strange and alien place, remote in miles from the home of old (it may be on the other side of the globe), or remoter still in character and circumstances. And we are meant not to ignore this locality, but to accept it, to enter into it, to sympathize with it, to submit, to love. But in order to do this aright we are called to remember our other and transcendent locality; we are "in Christ." Yes, quite as much as our Colossian brethren, quite as supernaturally as they, and quite as genuinely, we in our modern life (their life to them was as modern) are "joined to the Lord." Around us, in London, in Liverpool, in Cornwall, in India, in Canada, in China, in Africa, there lies the "surrounding" of Jesus Christ, for our life of faith and love, just where we are. Where we are, there is

He. With every call of every hour His word is, "*Let us* go hence."[1] And His companionship is not that *only* of the Companion; it is that of the Hiding-place, the Sanctuary, the enfolding Presence, the living and life-giving Head.

Lord Jesus Christ, enable us to recollect this with a quiet mind, to act upon it with a restful will; so shall we realize it ever more and more with a happy heart, full of thanksgiving to Thee.

---

[1] "'LET US GO HENCE.'

"And must we go? go from this quiet place,
  This paschal Chamber, where we listening rest,
  And hear Thy blessed voice, and see Thy face,
    And lean upon Thy breast?

"Go to that awful Garden? to these throngs
  Of midnight violence? to the unjust bar?
  To all the dreadful world's insulting wrongs
    And impious war?

"Yes, we can go, arising at Thy word;—
  Our sacred Place goes too, our vast Defence;
  For Thou hast said, Companion, Leader, Lord,
    'LET US go hence.'"

From the writer's book, *In the House of the Pilgrimage: Hymns and Sacred Songs* (Seeleys). The lines were suggested by a remark made to him by M. Théodore Monod, of Paris.

But let us follow the Apostle as he dictates. He is about to speak with joy of his knowledge, through Epaphras, that the converts, "in Colossæ," were indeed living "in Christ."

Ver. 3. **We are giving thanks to our** (τῷ) **God, the Father**[1] **of our Lord Jesus Christ, always, when praying on your behalf** (ὑπὲρ ὑμῶν, so read); approaching Him, as we so often do, in worshipping intercourse (προσευχόμενοι) about you, and "always," at such moments, filled first and most with thanksgiving for

Ver. 4. **His blessing manifested in you; having heard,** just now, from Epaphras, **of your faith in Christ Jesus,** of your reliance which rests anchored in Him, and of its outcoming effect, **the love which you have** (read ἣν ἔχετε) **to all the saints,** all your

Ver. 5. fellow-believers, near and far; **on account of the hope,** "that blessed Hope," the Return of your Lord, **laid up for you** in safe keeping (ἀποκειμένην) **in the heavens,** from which, in its season, it shall be manifested; the hope **which you heard of at the first**[2] **in the word,** the message, **of the truth of the**

---

[1] Probably omit καί before πατρι.

[2] Προηκούσατε: thus perhaps the προ- may be explained, as Bishop Lightfoot suggests. It contrasts (in this view) the *original* teaching of St Paul and his helpers with the unsound later "Gospel."

Gospel, that "good news" so infinitely superior to all man-originated speculations, that "authentic message of the skies" which in divine reality (ἀλήθεια) comes from above, instead of being a mere echo to voices from below; which Gospel has arrived among you (παρόντος εἰς ὑμᾶς), even as in the whole world besides (καί) it is fully bearing fruit,[1] and growing too;[2] for it is a plant whose growth is developed by its productiveness; even as it is doing too among you, ever since the day when you heard and came spiritually to know[3] the grace of God in its reality. Even as you

Ver. 6.

Ver. 7.

---

[1] Καρποφορούμενον. The middle voice somewhat adds to the force and fulness of the meaning of the verb; this may be conveyed by the rendering, "*fully* bearing fruit."—The reading best attested on the whole omits the word καί after ἐν παντὶ τῷ κόσμῳ, and thus allows of the rendering above: "in the whole world it is fruit-bearing."—It is scarcely necessary to point out that the words "in all the world" are hyperbolical, but not therefore untruthful, or even inexact; they exactly convey, under the well-known circumstances of the time, the meaning of the Apostle; they just state *with emphasis and energy* the vast diffusion of the Message in the Roman Empire.

[2] Καὶ αὐξανόμενον. This is to be added here to the Received Text, on ample documentary evidence.

[3] Ἐπέγνωτε. Almost always, by usage and connexion, ἐπιγινώσκειν in the N. T. means knowledge which goes deeper than the surface of facts; and so, continually, it is to be explained as the spiritual knowledge which *sees the truth in the fact, and finds the experience in the truth.*

learnt your lesson of salvation from **Epaphras, our beloved fellow-bondsman** in the sacred slavery of the Lord; **who is a faithful worker of Christ on our**
Ver. 8. **behalf;**[1] **who also informed us of your love in the Spirit;** the love resulting from that "love of God" which the Holy Spirit "poured out in your hearts" (Rom. v. 5), and which He maintains within you.

So the Epistle opens. Nothing could be more characteristic of St Paul, as regards thought, feeling, and expression. His heart and his mind are in every phrase, we may say in every word. It is entirely like him to feel, and to speak out, all this affection and all this honour for these converts to Christ, recent as they were at the longest, and his own children—in many cases his own grandchildren—in the faith. It is just like him to speak of Epaphras, though only in passing, in these terms of warm regard and personal grateful confidence, throwing himself wholly into his subordinate's life, and work, and pastoral

---

[1] Ὑπὲρ ἡμῶν. On the whole the evidence, documentary and internal together, is for this reading, and not for ὑπὲρ ὑμῶν.

joys. And it is just like St Paul to write of the Gospel as he does, to speak of it in "words that burn," to dwell with an intensity of soul which cannot be hid upon its supreme reality, its ἀλήθεια, and upon its blessed fulness of "fruit," its καρποφορία, as it traverses "the world" calling forth the golden harvest of faith, love, and hope at every step. All comes from the bright depths of that mighty but tender personality, the heart of the man whom the Lord had made so rich in the capacities of nature, and then had transfigured all through by revealing Himself to him, and taking possession of him in the new life.

And the *style* of the passage is eminently characteristic. The long sentence, in which clause flows out of clause without a break, all the way from εὐχαριστοῦμεν to ἀγάπην ἐν πνεύματι, is as Pauline as it well can be; the repeated καθώς, the "doubling back" of the thought where καθὼς καὶ ἐν ὑμῖν follows upon καθὼς καὶ ἐν παντὶ τῷ κόσμῳ. The individuality of the style, which puts into legible shape the personality of the man, is obvious to every one. We are certainly not allowed here to forget that the Scripture is human as well as divine. Paul is as truly in this paragraph as Sophocles is in the opening lines of the *Antigone*, or Bunyan in the closing scene of the *Pilgrim's Progress*. The Holy Ghost moved His vehicles to speak; but His vehicles were "holy *men* of God" (2 Pet. i. 21).

But then on the other side the "men" *were* His vehicles. And we turn to their words, as the Church from the first has turned, (taught by the Lord Jesus, who thus turned in His own sacred experience to the words of the Old Testament writers,) as to the Word of God. Let any one who pleases call this view of Scripture "a dead dogma"; it is as living a thing as the precept of Jesus Christ can make it, backed by His personal example.

So we take our paragraph, and ask not only what it tells us of the heart of a wonderful man, but what it says to us as the Word of life, our Master's own message, divine, direct, authoritative, to our souls.

As such, it has much to tell us, more

than I can even indicate here. It points out to us, for example, the glorious secret, eternally wonderful, of our sonship to God in Christ. "Grace and peace from God our Father"; "We are giving thanks to God, the Father of our Lord Jesus Christ." Let us read this again as if we had never read it before. When, long ago, some of the Danish missionaries in India set their educated converts to translate a catechism in which the Christian's privilege of sonship was expounded, one of the translators hesitated, and almost protested, at the boldness, the incredibility, of the words. "It is too much," he said; "let me rather render it, *They shall be permitted to kiss His feet.*" It would indeed be incredible, were it not revealed. "Behold, what manner of love!"

But the central and characteristic utterance of our paragraph lies in the fourth and fifth verses. There the Apostle, who, years before, had written to the Corinthians " the psalm of love" (1 Cor. xiii.), and at its close had grouped the blessed three, faith, hope, and love, to shine for ever together in Christian thought, recurs to the same theme, in the concrete example of the Colossians. He has heard of "their faith in Christ Jesus," and of "the love which they have to all the saints"; and he knows that this faith and this love have their life and energy "on account of the hope laid up for them in the heavens." Let us take the three words up for a simple meditation in brief detail.

i. "*Their* faith *in Christ Jesus*"; that is to say, (to repeat what we can never too distinctly recollect,) their souls' *reliance*, anchored in Him, resting in Him. (For such, as I undoubtedly take it, is the imagery of the phrase here, "*in* Christ Jesus."[1] It gives us the thought of reliance going forth to Christ, and reposing on Christ, so as to sink as it were into Him, and find fixture in Him; as the anchor sinks *to* the floor of the sea, and then *into* it, that it may be held *in* it.)

This comes first in the order; their faith, with its glorious Object—Christ Jesus. Not

---

[1] Πίστις, πιστεύειν, κ.τ.λ., are but rarely constructed with ἐν. But the idea conveyed is as intelligible, and valuable, as that conveyed by εἰς.

first their love, nor their hope, but first their faith—in Him. In other words, He must come first (in the ideal order) as the Object of their reliance; then He will be revealed fully and more fully for ever as the Object of their love, as it goes out to Him and to His members. Let us hold fast this principle; in the theology of our spiritual life, let us put first faith—that is to say, Christ relied upon. Let us not fall into the specious fallacy which would discredit faith in favour of love; with the almost inevitable result of discrediting a distinct, revealed, and infinitely *needed*, ground and warrant of faith, in favour of a religion of subjectivity and mere emotion. Faith, in the realities of the soul, is as needful to love as the fulcrum to the lever, or as the wick to the flame. Love indeed is "greater than" faith, from one glorious point of view; because faith is for the sake of love rather than love for the sake of faith. But who ever discredited the foundations of the Temple in favour of the Gate Beautiful, or thought that the Gate Beautiful could ever get beyond its need of the foundations? In the architect's thought the foundation was for the Gate, not the Gate for the foundation. But the foundation, vast, immoveable, planned with perfect skill, was majestically and for ever needful to the whole superstructure.

Christ the Object of faith gives faith all its value.[1] But the value of faith therefore is incalculable and eternal. For in practice it means just this, Christ relied upon by me a sinner, who immeasurably need Him. "Faith in Christ Jesus" is the soul's rest, underlying always all its true action.

ii. "*The* love *which they had to all the saints.*" If faith is the soul's rest, love is the soul's resultant action. I say resultant, for it is no less. If faith is faith indeed, if it is a genuine and practical reliance upon the revealed Lord Jesus Christ, then, in the spiritual nature of things, it must result in love. For it implies some sight of HIM. And as it goes on in its exercise and experience, relying on HIM, using HIM as Refuge, Strength, and Peace, it implies a genuine intercourse

---

[1] I venture to refer to the first chapter of a little book of mine, *Patience and Comfort* (Marshall, 1897).

with HIM. It implies a reception of Him into the intimacy of the soul. It opens the door to Him to "dwell in the heart, by faith" (see Eph. iii. 17). And the heart where the revealed and trusted Christ dwells *must* expand, and flow out of itself, to Him, and to others because of Him. It learns, because HE is there, in His practically experienced reality, to "find its delight in the felicity of others"; being itself possessed of such felicity in Him.

It is at rest; therefore it is both capacitated and animated to work. And its work is "the labour of love"; the sweet energies and sweet sympathies of a being which has found its ultimate safety and strength, and will migrate no more.

No wonder then that the Apostle, hearing of the "faith" of the Colossians, their "faith *in Christ Jesus*," heard also of their warm, practical, and comprehensive "love." Nor will it be a wonder that the connexion and sequence should be the like for us, by the grace of God. When are we most unselfish as Christians, most ready, most happy, to sympathize, to serve, to seek? When we are personally most at rest in faith. When we are most simply, most humbly, most freely, relying on the Lord Jesus, and finding Him to be to us " according to our faith," then, as never at other seasons, the heart swells with love to others, and rejoices to take the most useful line it can, whatever the line be, to shew it. When we are at rest *in Him*, the work of love is but the glad expression of our rest.

iii. " *On account of the* hope *laid up for them in the heavens.*" This phrase, " on account of," διά with the accusative, is noteworthy. It links closely together in a suggestive way " that blessed hope " (as it becomes an experience, reflecting itself in the believer's heart as the glad *feeling* of hope of the Lord's Coming and Glory) with the faith and love which have just been mentioned. Not that the hope is the *ground* of either the faith, or the love. But it is a grand *occasion* to develope them, and call them out into action. " Because of " that wonderful prospect, that promise that " Christ, which is our life, *shall appear*," " this same Jesus, in like manner "—because of that, and of all the bliss which it means to His disciples

—the believing heart believes more consciously and boldly, and the loving heart loves more gladly, and with a more heaven-like kindness of affection. In particular, with that hope in view, a peculiar warmth and sense of coherence comes into the "love towards all the saints." The thought of the one blessed goal, radiant with the light of the countenance of the coming King, draws nearer and nearer together the hearts of the scattered groups on all the paths of the pilgrimage towards it. The thought, the fact, the irrevocable promise, of "our gathering together *unto Him*," acts already, so far as it is allowed its full and natural force within us, to gather us together *unto one another*. St Peter makes beautiful use of this truth, though less obviously, in his First Epistle (v. 9), to animate tempted believers in faith's resistance to the tempter; he reminds them of their fellow-believers, *and of the common goal*; "whom resist, stedfast through your faith ($\sigma\tau\epsilon\rho\epsilon o\grave{\iota}$ $\tau\hat{\eta}$ $\pi\acute{\iota}\sigma\tau\epsilon\iota$, solid, impenetrable, because reliant on the Lord); as knowing that the same experiences of tribulations ($\tau\grave{\alpha}$ $\alpha\grave{\upsilon}\tau\grave{\alpha}$ $\tau\hat{\omega}\nu$ $\pi\alpha\theta\eta\mu\acute{\alpha}\tau\omega\nu$) are working towards the end, the goal (ἐπιτελεῖσθαι), for your world-scattered brotherhood (τῇ κατὰ κόσμον ὑμῶν ἀδελφότητι)."

Such is the life of faith, love, and hope, as "the word of the truth of the Gospel" sets it before us. It was lived at Colossæ then. It is "liveable," it is lived, in our world to-day. The secret transcends all time, for it is nothing less than the Lord Jesus Christ, blessed Object of reliance, love, and expectation, blessed inmost Reason and Power for a life of self-forgetting service, into which melancholy and isolation cannot enter, because of Him.

> "'Change and decay in all around I see;'
> So runs, as ever, earth's long mournful story
> But God's own truth, as ever, sets us free—
> A present Saviour, and a coming glory."

Hope, Christian soul; in every stage
Of this thine earthly pilgrimage
Let heavenly joy thy thoughts engage;
        Abound in hope.

Hope! for to all who meekly bear
Christ's cross, He gives His crown to wear;
Abasement here is glory there;
        Abound in hope.

Hope through the watches of the night;
Hope till the morrow brings thee light;
Hope till thy faith be lost in sight;
        Abound in hope.

B. H. Kennedy, D.D.

## THE APOSTLE'S PRAYER FOR THE COLOSSIANS

THERE can be little doubt but we shall find that our most successful hours of employment for our people were not those when we were speaking to them from God but when we were speaking for them to God.

C. BRIDGES, *The Christian Ministry.*

# CHAPTER III

### THE APOSTLE'S PRAYER FOR THE COLOSSIANS

#### COLOSSIANS i. 9-14

ST PAUL has told the Colossians of his joy over the good report of their spiritual state. Their faith, their love, their hope, have been depicted to him in warm colours by Epaphras; he can think of them all as richly supplied from their Lord's resources with all that makes the Christian life glad and fruitful. They are indeed "in the Spirit." Their love, which makes itself felt by "all the saints," is no mere transitory enthusiasm; it has its "environment," its vital air, in God; it is (ver. 8) "in the Spirit."

What will the Apostle do now? He is full of thanksgiving; but he cannot rest in even that. Just because he is so thankful he must at once go on to pray. Have the

Colossians so truly found life in the Name of Jesus Christ? Then he must at once ask that they may live it out in the right line. Have they received the power, the fire, of love, kindled in the golden lamp of faith? Then he must pray, with all his soul, that this power may be passed into the channel of the will of God, this flame may burn along the path of humble and happy obedience.

Ver. 9. **On account of this,** this recorded fact of your spiritual health and warmth, **we also,** we on our part, meeting your love with a love-prompted prayer, **ever since the day when we heard** the news from Epaphras, **never cease praying on your behalf,** seizing every occasion for prayer, and maintaining the *spirit* of prayer in literal continuity, **and requesting that you may be filled with the true, spiritual knowledge** (ἐπίγνωσις, more than γνῶσις [1]) **of His will,** the will of Christ (ver. 7); "filled" in the sense of a developed and entire insight into all its holiness, all its glory, and into the ways in which to meet it in practical life; **in all spiritual wisdom and intelligence;** "wisdom," the noble faculty of judging and acting aright, "intelligence," that faculty in

---

[1] See above, p. 32.

application to the living problems of the hour, and both "spiritual," for they are the effect of the Spirit's own work in you; **to walk** (perhaps, to set out walking, περιπατῆσαι, the aorist marking a new departure) **in a way worthy of the Lord** Christ; in a humble sense of "worthy," in the sense of recollecting what He is and how He has redeemed you; **to all meeting of His wishes** (ἀρέσκεια), so as not only to obey explicit precepts but as it were to anticipate in everything His "sweet, beloved will" always, everywhere[1]; **in every good work** (there must be no arbitrary selection and limitation in the field of His work set before you) **bearing fruit and growing with regard to** (read τῇ ἐπιγνώσει, the dative of reference) **the true spiritual knowledge of God**; for that knowledge has for one great law of its growth this, that we love and do His will, and bear the fruit of His Spirit. And our prayer includes a

Ver. 10.

---

[1] Ἀρέσκεια is an interesting and instructive word here "In classical Greek it denotes a cringing and subservient habit, ready to do anything to please a patron; not only to meet but to anticipate his most trivial wishes. But when transferred to . . . the believer's relations to his Lord the word at once rises by its associations. *To do anything* to meet, to anticipate, His wishes is not only the most beneficial but the most absolutely right thing we can do. It is His eternal due; it is at the same time the surest path to our own highest developement and gain" (Note here in the *Cambridge Bible for Schools, etc.*).—Cp. 1 Thess. iv. 1.

request for an ever-increasing strength in you for
Ver. 11. this blessed life, that you may be in **all
power empowered**, continuously, (the participle is
present, δυναμούμενοι,) **according to the might of His
glory**, on the scale of the resources of His manifested Nature (δόξα), which can amply pour force
into your weakness, with results above all in the
direction of love; **to all patience and longsuffering
with joy**; an issue not such as the world anticipates
from a gift of power, but which is just in character
with Him whose glory it is to forbear and to
forgive, while He is in all His holiness "the blissful,
the happy, God" (1 Tim. i. 11). And this life of
chastened but mighty joy will be of its own nature
a life of thanksgiving; so our prayer includes this
Ver. 12. for you, that you may live **giving thanks
to the Father** of our Lord, and of us in Him, **who
qualified us** to enter **on our** (τὴν) **portion of the lot of
the saints in the light**; "qualified" us by giving us,
in Christ, on whom we have believed, the title to
possess His blessings, those blessings which are as
it were the New Canaan of grace, divided among
the tribes of the New Israel, and in which they
and their inheritance are alike bright with "the
light of the Lord," "the light of the King's countenance," "the light of the glory of God in the
face of Jesus Christ." Yes, He has given us
"qualification" for that inheritance; and He has

given us also possession. He has not only told us that we have a title to our Canaan; He has carried

Ver. 13. us across the border: **who rescued us from the authority of the darkness,** that dread usurping dominion to which we had surrendered ourselves in our fallen state, the dominion of the powers of the spiritual night, with its delusion, pollution, and death, **and transferred us into the Kingdom of the Son of His love,** this same blessed "lot of our inheritance," this Canaan of grace, but now viewed as the Kingdom of the true David. It is no land of licence miscalled liberty, but full of the holy order and subjection of obedient love, love to "the Son of the love of the Father," the Son on whom eternally descends the ocean-stream of the infinite Affection, which comes on us also as we are in

Ver. 14. Him; **in whom,** united to whom in covenant and life, **we possess our** ($\tau\dot{\eta}\nu$) **redemption,** our ransom, our deliverance by the wonderful way of law, of purchase, of emancipation, because of the infinite value of His sacrifice;[1] a redemption which is in fact just this, as to its great primary element (immeasurably humbling to man, and glorifying to God)—**the remission, the forgiveness, of our sins.**

---

[1] The words in the Received Text διὰ τοῦ αἵματος αὐτοῦ should be omitted; they were probably inserted by copyists from the closely parallel passage, Eph. i. 7. But the thought of them is present in the context; see ver. 20 below.

So closely is this introductory passage woven, so continuous is the strain of its deep music, that it is very difficult to make a lawful pause even here.  The words on which we do now pause are full of movement still; they are as it were in act to rise and swell into the great paragraph which follows, and in which the surpassing personal glory of the Son of God shines out unveiled.  But I venture, almost arbitrarily, to reckon this the full-stop, and to ask the reader to stand still with me here and look back and look round upon the treasures we have touched.

The messages to the soul are many in these six verses.  The first and the most comprehensive of them is the message of the motive of the Apostle's prayer for the Colossians. He and Timotheus, he says, are very much in prayer for them; so much so that, with a hyperbole which is perfectly truthful to the heart, he speaks of the petitions as "incessant." They are the outcome of a great desire, a deep consciousness of a real occasion, a need for which the supplies of God are urgently required.  And what is the need?  Are the

Colossians so low and so cold in spiritual life? Is everything on the decline? No; it is the very opposite. They are so full of faith, hope, and love, "love in the Spirit. They have such a noble fruit-bearing capacity; they are in a condition of such vigorous growth. *Therefore* he prays for them, as well as gives thanks. For the state in which they are has inevitably, with its blessings, its risks also. It is the very state in which a lack of direction may bring loss, if not disaster. The sails are set so full that the need of compass and rudder is the more pressing. Let the warm and loving community begin to live its spiritual life on the wrong line, let it get into wrong convictions about the will of God, the work of Christ, the manifestation of holiness, and it may follow those convictions to all the greater lengths for the initial energy in which they were taken up.

So he prays for them, as for souls in need, that they may before everything else " be filled with *the true knowledge* of the will of God." He asks first that they may advance in the "wisdom and intelligence" of the spiritual life; that they may be, under the guidance of the Holy Ghost, men of balanced minds and quick discernment, not soon carried away by specious counterfeits of truth; quick to see the bearings of doctrine and duty. He asks that their practical conduct may be such as is "worthy of *the Lord*"; always regulated by the fact that they have a Master, a King, who has saved them, and whose will, definite and revealed, is to be their law. They are not to be content with the warm consciousness of religious emotions; they are to live their spiritual life in the line of a Master's orders. Nay more, they are so to fill their thoughts with Him, with Him as Master, that they shall delight to anticipate His *words* by the loyal study of His *mind*, going out to meet Him in a noble "eagerness to please." He prays that the Colossians may be always *practically* pious, "bearing fruit in every *good work*," never content with theory and reverie; and that so they may grow in that true knowledge of their God which no reveries apart from obedience can ever bring. And then he prays that every access of spiritual power, flowing out of His secret source, may express itself above all things in ways which shew the dethronement of self-will; in perseverance under trial (ὑπομονή), in longsuffering under provocation (μακροθυμία), and in the joy (χαρά) of "a heart at leisure from itself" and occupied with Christ. He prays finally that this joy may take continually the fair form of thanksgiving for the wonder, the miracle, of their salvation. May their happy thoughts tend steadily that way; occupied with the Father's free gift of sonship in His family, and of wealth in His Canaan, partnership with all saints in the Holy Land of grace, under the unsetting Sun of Love; never forgetting how their God sent to seek them in the dark Egypt of the Fall and brought them over to be the blessed subjects, the ennobled vassals, of His own Beloved One. May they recollect that to that King they not only belong as subjects; they are joined to Him as limbs; "in Him," and in Him alone, they no longer seek only but possess "the redemption," the ransom and release, of a wonderful, an abundant, pardon.

"Beware," some one has said, "of an

untheological devotion." The sentence may be distorted to mean what is absurd. But rightly taken it is a word of truth and wisdom. By "untheological" is intended what is baseless, unauthorized, unreasoned; a "devotion" which is careless of its ground, its revealed warrant, and also of the true glory of its Object. And the caution has reference to the fact that such "untheological devotion" has a natural tendency either to evaporate or to degenerate; worship can be kept both pure and warm only by being kept in watchful contact with its true Object and Reason.

St Paul has here just such a thought in view. This noble passage, this prayer in solemn detail for these living and loving souls, is no mere exercise of sacred rhetoric. It has to do with the joy he feels over Colossæ, but also with the fears he has about the permanence of its blessings. He dreads the prospect of an alien teaching and influence laying hold of this fine material and moulding it all awry. And so he tells them that he is praying for them, and asking just these "theological" blessings;—a growth in spiritual wisdom, in the knowledge of God, in a temper chastened self-wards and rejoicing God-wards; a perpetual thankfulness for a salvation nobly "theological," in which they shall bless their Father and their Redeemer for no vague and indefinite mercies, but for endowment and covenant under which they stand rescued from a tremendous evil and constituted the lawful vassals of their atoning King. He prays that they may not only be warm and earnest, but may know profoundly the reason of their hope. He prays above all that their "theological devotion" may get immortal life and strength from this, that it is all related to an infinitely blessed Person, the Son of the Father's love, and to the Father through Him.

So thinking, so worshipping, they would be happy, but they would also be forearmed. They would not lightly then be "beguiled of their reward." The specious counterfeits of truth would find from them no indolent and unsuspicious welcome; they would *miss* in the "other gospel" the well-understood characteristics of the old; and they would know that the old was better.

This prayer of St Paul's, thus read in the context of the Epistle, is no untimely message for us. In many quarters of our Christendom nothing is more in fashion than "an untheological devotion." "The religious sentiment" is regarded far and wide as a thing which can live and be healthy with a very *minimum* of revelation, and with an almost *nil* of reasoned doctrine; above all of the doctrine of a divine Christ, an atoning Cross, and a rescue from "the authority of the darkness." But such "sentiment," however warm, has no ultimate "last" in it. Under very moderate pressure from fashions of thought, and from attractive personalities, it is ready to go as far as possible from the ground on which alone the world, the flesh, and the devil can be really met.

Let us pray for ourselves, and for others, "in these dangerous days," along the line of this apostolic prayer. Let us pray for nothing short of a growth in the knowledge of God, and of a thanksgiving to the Father who has given us, in His Son, the forgiveness of our sins, and the radiant Canaan of His grace. Let us pray that above all we may be continually preoccupied against all that is really alien to peace and holiness, by being occupied with the SAVIOUR of our souls, in His Person, His work, His love, His glory. Would we be protected beforehand against the malaria of misbelief? Let us cultivate true joy in the true Lord.[1]

So far we have noticed the message conveyed to us by this paragraph as a whole—the message of the motive of the Apostle's prayer for the Colossians. Let us now turn to certain points of detail. Apart from its general context, the prayer conveys to us some truths of the first order.

i. Observe then the implied precept of that petition, " that you may walk in a way worthy of the Lord, to all meeting of His wishes," εἰς πᾶσαν ἀρέσκειαν. In a note to the paraphrase there I spoke about the proper meaning of the Greek word, and its bad and ignoble connexions in the classics; and then of the

---

[1] I venture to refer to my *Philippian Studies*, ch. viii., for further remarks in this direction, occasioned by the exposition of Phil. iii. 1.

magic with which the Gospel has transfigured it. I touch it again only to point out how it suggests to us the intended intimacy and endearment of the relation of wish and will between the believer and the Lord. We are meant, in the light of this transfigured word, ἀρέσκεια, to think of His will as an *affectionate* servant thinks of the wishes (not merely of the spoken or written-down orders) of the master, or the mistress, who has made the house of service a genuine home, and has almost hidden authority away in friendship. Even such an illustration scarcely satisfies the case. This "anticipatory obedience" is rather to be that of a devoted son to a parent,[1] to a loving and beloved parent, to whom perhaps the son has not been always dutiful. How can he now do enough to undo that lamented past? How can he too much try, and delight, to obliterate the scars of past neglect by a present studious and watchful "meeting of the wishes"?

---

[1] Not that we ought ever unreservedly to compare our Saviour to a Father. He is distinctively the Elder Brother. But there are elder brothers in common life whose love and goodness command filial thoughts from their juniors.

In a singularly beautiful passage in the fine *Prologue to the Satires*, Pope speaks of the watch he keeps over his aged mother's happiness; how it is his delight to

> "Explore the wish, explain the asking eye,
> And save awhile one parent from the sky."

That first line is exactly the "anticipation of the will" of which St Paul speaks here; only it is glorified by its application not to a mother's old age but to the even nobler object of a Redeemer's unseen presence. Shall it be so between us and Him? Shall we not "*explore* His wish"? Shall we disappoint the 'asking eye" which is "upon us" (Ps. xxxii. 8: "Mine eye upon thee," Heb.), and whose condescending love *does* even "ask" us to serve and please? Have we not often disappointed it in the past? Shall we not now more than meet it, especially in the small, passing things in which love may be so easily slighted, so tenderly met and served?

ii. Then we take particular note of that other bright detail of the passage, in ver. 11; "in all power empowered according to the might of His glory, to all patience and long-suffering with joy." This is one of several Pauline passages which put before us the beautiful paradox of holy power coming out in holy gentleness. The amplest of all these passages is that in Ephesians, where the third chapter ends and the fourth begins. The third chapter leads us deep into the great fountains of life and power in the heart of the Rock of Ages. We see the Christian " strengthened by the Spirit in the inner man," and receiving Christ into his very heart, and " filled, up to all the fulness of God," and living upon Him who can do far, far " more than we ask or think, according to His power working in us." The words cannot go further in presenting to us the more than gigantic forces which are provided for us in our union and communion with God in Christ. But how are those forces to be used? Is the Christian, in contact with this "giant's strength," to "use it like a giant"?[1] No; he is to use it like a Christian.

---

[1] "O it is excellent
To have a giant's strength, but it is tyrannous
To use it like a giant."
*Measure for Measure*, ii. 2.

How does the fourth chapter of Ephesians begin? With an "entreaty" from "the prisoner of the Lord," on the very account of what he has just said, to "walk worthy of the calling in all lowliness and meekness, with longsuffering, forbearing one another in love, striving to keep the oneness of the Spirit in the bond of peace." The "giant's strength" is to be used, first and most, upon and against self-will, self-pleasing, self-assertion, self-advertisement; it is to be turned in upon all that contradicts love; and then it is to be poured out along the line of love. So it is to be used in a way exactly unlike that of the "giant" of the poet's words.

In a briefer but not less pregnant form the same precious truth in paradox is here. Very probably this verse, Col. i. 11, is the germ of the more developed passage, Eph. iii., iv., which was written just later. What words, even in Eph. iii., are much stronger than these as to the "giant's strength" which is for us in the "Stronger than the strong"? "Empowered in all power—according to, on the scale of, the might of His glory"; in a sense and in a measure calculated by that wonderful source,

"His glory," His nature in its manifested splendour of life and love! And this, *continuously*; so the Greek tells us, with its present participle, δυναμούμενοι. We need fear no exhaustion, as if a single great deposit were given us, and we might now be getting near its end. No; our "Rock follows us." The secret of power is continually at our side. As the occasions rise, we are to draw again, and again, and always, from its waters, which stand always at the brim. And then—what is to be the resultant stream? Not, primarily, a rush of energies, a torrent of witness, a blaze of miracles, a life which is to "make history" in the world's sense of the words. It is to be "unto all patience and longsuffering, with joy." The life is to be deep and strong with that "patience" which means a calm persistency in doing and bearing the will of God; and with that "longsuffering" which means the power to meet "the provoking of all men" with a heart free from itself and bound to the Lord of love; and with that "joy" which means living, conscious, absolute satisfaction in Him.

The wonderful "power" is to be the power which overwhelms the life of self, and shines with the love of God in intercourse with man. Shall we not here also pray in the line of St Paul's petition, first for ourselves, then for the whole Church of Christ? And as we pray we will humbly open our hands to the Promiser, to receive.

iii. Again, we observe in the prayer that pregnant phrase which throws the light of glory upon the life of grace; " He qualified us to enter on our portion of the lot of the saints in the light." The words read at first sight as if they must mean, simply, heaven; the light of the countenance of "the King in His beauty," in "the land that is very far off." And they are fully worthy of the reference; if in hymn, or prayer, or exhortation, we ever find them so applied, let us welcome and use the application. Nevertheless, the immediate context may assure us that they refer properly to the believer's position and possession "even now." This Canaan is not in the distance, beyond death; it is about us to-day, in our home, in our family, in our business, in our worship, in our company, in our solitude, in our joys, in our tears, in all that makes up mortal life. This "light" is not the glow of the sky as it is stretched above the hills of immortality; it falls upon the plains of time; it is shed around the trying, the commonplace, the exhausting pathway of to-day. What is the Canaan? It is "the Kingdom of the Son" of God. And we are in it, for we are in Him. What is the light, the sunshine? It is the glory of the Father's love, without a cloud. And we are in "the Son of His love."

Already, "Christ is Paradise," to the disciple who believes and loves. Already we are called to "walk in the light, as He is in the light," and to "have fellowship with one another," He with us, we with Him. Shall this too be our material for prayer—and for reliant and receiving faith?

iv. Lastly, and in fewest words, our paragraph has a message straight to the primary need of us sinners. "In Him we have our redemption, the forgiveness of sins." There we evermore go back in recollection, and in faith, amidst all the blessings which are meant to anticipate glory itself in the fulness of grace. In this wonderful Canaan, in the Kingdom of the Son, delivered from the dark dominion of the Egypt of spiritual death, we need still, we seek still, we *have* still, that humbling but most precious and purifying gift, the forgiveness of our sins. And it, like everything else, is ours " in HIM."

Who can fathom the abyss
   Where Thou plunged'st for our love?
Who conceive the glorious bliss
   Waiting on Thy steps above?

    \*     \*     \*     \*

Lord, when we recall the story
Of Thy lowliness and glory,
Keep us, lest we fall from Thee,
Through that awful mystery.

ANSTICE.

*THE PRE-EMINENCE OF THE SON OF GOD*

O UNEXAMPLED love,
Love nowhere to be found less than divine!
Hail, Son of God, Saviour of men! Thy name
Shall be the copious matter of my song
Henceforth, nor ever shall my harp Thy praise
Forget, nor from Thy Father's praise disjoin.

MILTON.

## CHAPTER IV

### THE PRE-EMINENCE OF THE SON OF GOD

COLOSSIANS i. 15-20

THE Prayer of St Paul for the Colossians, or rather, his account of it to them, is now over, at least in the sense of explicit petitions. He has told them what he has been asking for them; an always clearer insight into the will of God, a tenderer love of it, a life whose tone is deeply chastened, while happy, just because of the divine power at its heart, and a spirit of warmer thanksgiving to the blessed Father, in view of an assured part and lot in the Canaan-kingdom of His Son.

The prayer has no formula of conclusion, no ascription and Amen. It closes by rising without a break into the utterance of a wonderful *Credo*, a worshipping and enraptured confession of the glory of the Christ of God, whose Person has filled the last phrases of the prayer.

This Creed of Christ's Pre-eminence, if I may call it so, is a passage of the highest possible importance for Christian Doctrine. It gives us some great fundamental *data* for a believing Theology of both the Person and the Work of the Lord. And it was undoubtedly written with a definitely doctrinal purpose; it recites the wonders of what "the Son of the Father's love" is, in His eternity, in His relation to the Universe, in His relation to the Church, with a manifest regard to the alien teaching which was invading Colossæ. Whatever that teaching was from other sides, it was, as regarded Christ, the Christ of Salvation, a theory minimizing, derogatory, and in that sense hostile. As we have seen (ch. i.), it depreciated His Person, by beclouding it with a pantheon of almost rival angel-powers. And it depreciated His work, by insisting on a ceremonial connexion and a certain ascetic discipline, in order to supplement and as it were support His salvation. Such tendencies the Apostle meets here first by this assertion, this confession, of the unapproachable pre-eminence of Jesus Christ from every point of view.

But let us not think only of the dogmatic occasion and direction of the passage. For surely as it rose in the soul and the mind of its writer it was immensely much to *him*, as well as a great message to others. Can we read it, and not feel that it glows and moves with a personal "joy in believing"? He is not only discoursing, still less discussing; he is worshipping. Upon his own heart this Lord Jesus Christ is rising and shining, in all His majesty, and mercy, and necessity, and infinitely fair beauty. St Paul is writing for Colossæ, but it is about a Lord whom he is beholding for himself; "in Him believing, he rejoices, with joy unspeakable and full of glory."

It is thus that the Bible always gives us its theology. The divine Book is full of articulate and reasoned statements of eternal verities about God, and Christ, and man. It puts these things into forms which are both models and powerful stimulants for religious thought and teaching as scientific (if the word may be used) as possible. Age after age Scripture has occasioned, it has demanded, from the deepest and acutest minds all the attention they can give in order worthily to analyse, arrange, and expound, its dogmatic contents. A French thinker, himself not a believer in Christianity, has affirmed his conviction that the scientific study of the *data* of the Christian Creed has been the most powerful of all the elements in the education of the European mind. Yet the Book which presents those *data*, and presents them so often in forms of great completeness as regards reasoning and expression, never (may I not say never?) presents them merely as in a lecture, or a treatise. They are all passed through the heart. The dogmatic prediction is shaped in the very soul, usually the suffering soul, of the seer who utters it. The dogmatic exposition is written down by a teacher who as it were writes upon his knees, and looks up continually from his argument to worship the Subject of it, with love, and joy, and tears. It is so here. It is so in such passages as Rom. iii.-viii., and 1 Cor. xv., and the whole Epistle to the Hebrews, and the First Epistle of St John. All is oracle. But the human heart, new-created by the Lord, and filled with Him, is the temple where this oracle is delivered. And we who so receive our oracles of eternal truth and life are bound to carry them away and use them in a spirit worthy of their origin. Our creed is never to be a mere code of propositions in the abstract. It is to breathe and glow, even where it is most systematic, with the Christian's own experience of worship, rest, and joy, in full sight of the glory of Him who has loved him and has died for him.

Let us follow the Apostle's thought then as it rises through prayer into worshipping confession.

Ver. 15. **Who is Image of God, the Unseen God;** whether in the heavenly world,[1] or in ours, it is in

---

[1] So the context indicates. The reference is not *only* to the visibility of the Lord Incarnate, but to His being always and everywhere, eternally, the Manifestation of the Father.

Him that the Father is beheld as He is; **Firstborn over all creation,**[1] Himself "not created but begotten," the SON, the HEIR of all things, and thus eternally antecedent to all contingent and created being; as is seen when we ponder His relation to it;

Ver. 16. **because in Him** (ἐν αὐτῷ : certainly not "*by* Him") **were created,** constituted in existence, ἐκτίσθη,[2] **all things that are** (τὰ πάντα)—yes, "in Him," as the Effect is in its Cause ;—in Him lay eternally the power and the law of their becoming and being[3] ;

---

[1] Πρωτότοκος πάσης κτίσεως : the words can of course be rendered "Firstborn of all creation," and this would (on the surface) seem to mean, "Created, and so belonging to creation; only, created before all other creatures." But the immediate following context is clearly against such a meaning, for it aims manifestly to *difference* the Son of God from all created things; they were "created *in* Him, *through* Him, and *for* Him." The genitive κτίσεως thus invites us to explain it as a genitive of relation: "Firstborn in His relation to the κτίσις"; *i.e.* the First born of the Eternal, His great Son and Heir, One with Him in Being and Glory; and thus related to the created Universe as (*a*) its Antecedent, (*b*) its Lord.—Cp. Ps. lxxxix. 27, "I will make Him My Firstborn." The Rabbis, in view of that passage, gave the title "Firstborn" to Messiah, and the Alexandrian Philo used a similar word of his mysterious "Logos."

[2] Κτίζειν does not *per se* mean "to bring into being out of nothing" (save the creative Will). But by connexion and usage it can denote this; like the Hebrew *bárá*.

[3] "A meaning more recondite has been seen here . . . that the Son, the Logos, is as it were the archetypal Universe, the Sphere and Summary of all finite being as it existed . . . in

all things, I say, **in the heavens and on the earth,**[1] that is to say, in all regions of created existence, **the visible things and the invisible,** alike worlds and personalities, and now particularly the personalities of the superhuman sphere, **whether thrones, or lordships, or governments, or authorities,** whatever be the ranks and orders of the hierarchy of the Unseen, and whether they be the powers who stood, or the powers who fell from "their first estate"[2]; **all things that are** (τὰ πάντα) **stand created** (ἔκτισται, perfect),

---

the Eternal Mind, and accordingly that, when it came into being in time, its 'creation' was 'in' Him who thus summed it up. . . . Such a view is rather read into the words . . . from non-Christian philosophies than derived from the words" (*Cambridge Bible for Schools, etc.*).—Some important matter on this point will be found in Dr J. H. Rigg's work, *Modern Anglican Theology.*

[1] Read ἐν τοῖς οὐρανοῖς καὶ ἐπὶ τῆς γῆς, not τὰ ἐν . . . τὰ ἐπί.

[2] It seems clear to me that St Paul is here alluding to these celestial ranks as realities, not as creations of the imagination which he would sweep away out of thought. In a context like this, where everything is meant to exalt the glory of the Son of God, he would surely put Him before us as the creative Cause not of imaginary but of real hosts and powers. That St Paul may, and probably does, include the now *rebel* spirits is clear from e.g. Eph. vi. 12.—Theories of angelic orders appear early in Christian and semi-Christian literature, but are fully developed in the *Celestial Hierarchy*, written (cent. v. or vi.) under the name of Dionysius the Areopagite. From his enumeration Milton borrowed his majestic line,

"Thrones, Dominations, Princedoms, Virtues, Pow'rs."

See note on Eph. i. 22 in the *Cambridge Bible for Schools, etc.*

constituted in existence, **by means of Him** (δι' αὐτοῦ) as the sublime Agent of the Father, **and unto Him** (εἰς αὐτόν), so that their final cause is to serve His will, to contribute to His glory; He who is their Creator is also their Goal.[1] Their whole being, willingly or unwillingly, moves that way—to Him; whether, as His blissful servants, they shall be as it were His throne; or, as His stricken enemies,

Ver. 17. "His footstool." **And He**, HE in emphasis (αὐτός), **is before all things**; IS, not only was; with a being before because above all time; **and these** (τά) **"all things" in Him are held together** (συνέστηκε); He is not their Cause only, in an initial sense; He is for ever their Bond, their Order, their Law, the ultimate Secret which makes the whole Universe, seen and unseen, a Cosmos, not a Chaos.[2]

Thus far the adoring Theologian has glorified and expounded the Son of God in His relation to Creation, to Nature, to the Universe. Have we listened to him with a full apprehension of the grandeur and significance of the utterance? And have we appreciated its

---

[1] Bishop Lightfoot.
[2] Bishop Lightfoot. "The declaration ... is in fact tantamount to 'in Him they live, and move, and have their being'" (Bishop Ellicott).

wonder, as we remember of Whom he speaks —the Being who so recently had lived in a Galilean town, and suffered a violent death (as we are reminded a few verses below) outside the walls of Jerusalem? This is an aspect of New Testament Christology always surprising and impressive. The Apostles never for a moment forget the historical life and death of their Master; they say so much about it that from their Epistles, and their discourses in the Acts, we can reconstruct a tolerable outline of the story of the Gospels. How could it be otherwise, when those "days of the Son of Man" were well within the adult experience of people who were only elderly when this Epistle was written? Yet in the same breath, and without the slightest apparent strain or effort, they speak of Him, they deal with Him, as the Lord of heaven and earth, nay, in this passage, as the infinite Cause and adequate End of all finite existence. And this transcendent view of the Person whose biography in Palestine yet lies so clear, and so near, to their eyes, is no excrescence of their thought, or intrusion into it; it conditions their whole character, it animates, governs, sanctifies, glorifies their being, while it leaves it perfectly sane and sober in the midst of human life.

There is no real accounting for such a creed, *so held, and so lived*, except on the one theory that it was the expression of a fact, the supreme fact of all, that " the Son, which is the Word of the Father, begotten from everlasting of the Father, very and Eternal God," " for us men and for our salvation came down from heaven, and was incarnate, and was made Man, and suffered for us, and rose again."[1] Blessed be His Name, to which every knee shall bow.

In passing, let us remember the pregnant import of this passage, in which the Son is revealed to us[2] as Cause, Head, and Goal of the created Universe. How much it has to say to us! For one thing, it binds both " worlds," the seen and unseen, the material and spiritual, into one, under one Head. And this is a precious gain when our hearts fail us on the border-line between the two.

---

[1] Art. ii. of the English Church, and the " Nicene " Creed.

[2] To a degree unexampled even in St Paul's Epistles. John i. and Heb. i. are the only adequate parallels.

For another thing, it sanctifies "Nature" to us, and makes its immeasurable heights and depths at once safe and radiant with the Name of Jesus Christ. It connects the remotest æon of the past with Him. It connects the remotest star detected by the photographic plate with Him. It bids us, when we feel as if lost in the enormity of space and time, fall back upon the Centre of both—for that centre is our Lord Jesus Christ, who died for us. In Him they hold together. He knows all about them; the mystery of space, the mystery of time, great to us, are no mysteries to Him. Looking on Him, and then on the beautiful but awful sky of stars, we can say with the poet,[1]

"Spirit, nearing yon dark portal at the limit of thy human state,
 Fear not thou the hidden purpose of that Power which alone is great,
 Nor the myriad world, His shadow, nor the silent Opener of the Gate."

With another,[2] whose harp rung still truer

---

[1] Tennyson, *God and the Universe.*
[2] Cowper, *The Winter Walk at Noon.*

to the eternal things, we can rejoice to think that

> "All things are under One. One Spirit, His
> Who wore the platted thorns with bleeding brows,
> Rules universal Nature."

With His Name the traveller can rejoice in the glories of mountain, forest, and flood, worshipping not Nature but Christ its Cause and End; Artificer of the landscape, while He is Saviour of the soul. With that same dear Name the explorer of physical secrets can consecrate his laboratory, remembering that Christ is the ultimate Law of compound and cohesion, while He is the Saviour of the soul. "The Lord shall rejoice in His works"; and man may indeed do so likewise, the more, not the less, because, if he is regenerate and believing man, his ultimate and spiritual "joy is in the Lord" (Ps. civ. 31, 34).

But the Apostle has by no means done with his blessed theme. He has seen Christ supreme in Nature. Now the same Christ appears as the Fountain-depth out of which comes the life eternal in the sphere of Grace.

Ver. 18. **And He,** HE again, with the same solemn emphasis (αὐτός), **is,** IS again, with the same suggestion of an eternal fact, **the Head of the Body;** His Body, conditioned as such by relation to His Headship; that is to say, **the Church,** "the blessed company of all faithful people," the Congregation whom grace has drawn into living contact with Him[1]; He is the Head, as He is supremely qualified to be, **seeing He is** (ὅς ἐστιν), in His essential Character, **Origin** (ἀρχή), Life-source, **Firstborn from among the dead,** even as He is eternally "Firstborn" (ver. 15) in His relation to the Universe. I say, "from the dead," for, wonderful to say, He, this Lord of Life, has passed actually through death; in order to become Head of His Church He needed not only to be born but to die, and to take His life again, the same yet other, an "indissoluble life"; **that He might become in all things,** in grace as in nature, in salvation as in

---

[1] "As presented here, the idea [of the Church] rises above the level of 'visibility'; it transcends human registration and external organization, and has to do supremely with direct spiritual relations between the Lord and the believing Company.... All other meanings of the word Church are derived and modified by this, but this must not be modified by them. See Hooker, *Eccl. Polity*, iii. 1" (Note in the *Cambridge Bible for Schools, etc.*).—The late Rev. E. A. Litton's treatise on *The Church* is highly instructive on many aspects of the subject.

creation, even **He** (αὐτός), **the holder of the Primacy** (πρωτεύων); from every point of view PRE-EMINENT.

"That in all things He might have the pre-eminence." "And He must have it; and He will have it; and He shall have it!" The words were uttered by the Rev. C. Simeon, in his pulpit at Cambridge, in his old age, about the year 1835. The scene was reported to me from memory in 1868 by the late Dean Howson, of Chester; he was in the church, and heard the impassioned words, and saw the form of the aged preacher actually rise in height as the soul erected the body to bear witness to the Redeemer's glory. The effect was strong and thrilling. But the words and action were after all only the *just* utterance of a faithful servant consenting from his heart to *the fact* of his Lord's glory, and of his Father's purpose for the Son of His love. So let our hearts take them up to-day. For the Universe, for the Church, Christ is and must be "pre-eminently" the First, the Head. And therefore this He must be, He will be, He shall be, not only to the world and the

Church but to me the creature of His will, the believer in His promise.

"The Head of the Body." This is His "pre-eminence" with relation to His people. In that word Head much lies involved. It betokens of course primacy of authority; the right of supreme direction. Over "His Body" the Son of God, Incarnate, Sacrificed, Glorified, absolutely presides; and so over every limb of His body; and so over my reader, and over me. In everything, at every moment, I am under my Head, Christ (1 Cor. xi. 3). He is my Sovereign, and I His vassal, His bondservant, His implement, to the uttermost. The more entirely I recognize this, and the more I love it, the greater the freedom and the less the friction of my life. But along with all this, the word "Head" tells me that He is my life as well as my law; my secret of energy, my power to do His will. He lives in me; He carries out His glorious life, in true measure, through me. And in that fact there lies an inexhaustible secret of rest and strength for the "limb" as it yields itself to the orders of its Head. And as for the limb, so for the whole organism :

> "To know, to do the Head's commands,
> For this the Body lives and grows;
> All speed of feet, all skill of hands,
> Is for Him spent *and from Him flows.*"

It is to the Epistles to Colossæ and Ephesus that we owe the whole *express* revelation of the Headship of Christ. Let us prize these Epistles, if for this gift alone.

But St Paul has more to say. Our glorious Head is to be set before us further as He is constituted for His wonderful office in the eternal purpose.

Ver. 19. **For in Him**, this Son of His love, **He**, the **Father**,[1] **was pleased**, in the eternal, timeless, "good

---

[1] Ὅτι ἐν αὐτῷ ηὐδόκησε πᾶν τὸ πλήρωμα κατοικῆσαι. Grammatically, we may explain this in three ways; (*a*) "For in Him all the Plenitude was pleased to dwell"; (*b*) "For He (Christ) was pleased that all the Plenitude should dwell in Him"; (*c*) "For He (the Father) was pleased, etc.," as above. On the whole the last seems preferable, as the next verses go on, in the same construction, to speak of the same Agent in a way which manifestly points to the Father. So A.V., R.V., and all the older English versions, the Rhemish excepted.

pleasure" which drew the plan of our redemption, that **all the Plenitude**, the Plenitude of the Godhead (ii. 9), "the totality of the divine Powers and Attributes,"[1] **should take up its lasting abode** (κατοικῆσαι, aorist); *beginning* that Residence, *from the point of view of our salvation*,[2] when He came
Ver. 20. to Incarnation and Atonement. **To proceed** (καί); the Father was pleased, **by means of Him**, the Son, **to reconcile**, to provide amnesty and welcome for, **all things unto** Him, the Father, **making peace**, between Himself and His fallen creatures, **by means of the blood of His Cross**, the Cross of the Son, where the Son was "made a curse for us, to buy us out from under the curse of the law" (Gal. iii. 13), as "the Propitiation for our sins" (1 John ii. 2); by means of that sacred blood which signifies and embodies His vicarious death, with its immeasurable

---

[1] Bishop Lightfoot. See his Essay (*Colossians*, pp. 323, etc., ed. i.) on the meaning of πλήρωμα, of which the true idea is "the filled condition of a thing," and so, a realized ideal. The word was technical in the Jewish schools, and connected with the eternally realized Ideal of Godhead.

[2] From the point of view of the Eternal Sonship the πλήρωμα *is* eternally in the Son; it does not "take up" its abode in Him as if it had to begin. But that surely is not in view here. Practically, the meaning is that He, in the great crisis of Redemption, came to be "God *manifest in flesh*," God Incarnate.

merits. I say, "all things,"[1] **whether the things upon the earth, or the things in the heavens,** that is to say, the human and the angelic worlds alike; the human world in the sense so fully understood in the Gospel of our salvation from guilt and sin, the angelic world in a sense known as yet only to the Lord. But it is assuredly connected with the mysterious fact that it also was once invaded by sin and rebellion, and that the heavenly temple itself therefore somehow needed a cleansing effect to fall upon it from the Cross.

Not without significance, surely, there is no mention here of " the things under the earth," the phrase of Phil. ii. 11. The world of loss is indeed in some undiscovered sense to " confess that Jesus Christ is Lord "; and that is an assurance which has in it, if we may say so, an awful peace. But it is not the same thing as the purpose and promise of " reconciliation." Let us not read into this passage what is not here, and is not anywhere in Scripture, an absolute universalism, a " larger hope "

---

[1] The words δι' αὐτοῦ before εἴτε τὰ ἐπὶ τῆς γῆς, in the *Textus Receptus*, should be omitted. They may have been a transcriber's insertion to aid the reader in tracing the connexion.

which is ultimately to neutralize the most formidable warnings. Let us be sure that God will be for ever and everywhere HIMSELF in His whole character; that He will never and nowhere be inequitable and unmerciful. But let us pray for a holy fear, deep and awful; let us " flee from the wrath to come."

Once more the Apostle's great flight of worshipping thought pauses, not to alight but as it were to hover while it prepares for a new movement. As it stays, let us rest awhile, in wonder and in faith. Let us take another long look upwards at this blessed Son of the Father's love, Cause and Corner-stone of the Universe, visible and invisible, Head of the Church, giving law to His Body, and giving it also a law-fulfilling power. Behold Him; He is Tabernacle for ever of the eternal Plenitude, Bearer in His Incarnation of Godhead itself, and therefore infinite Fountain for us of every resource which we need for life and holiness. And then let us make haste again to the foot of the Cross. Let us see this most mysterious Being nailed there with nails, and crowned with thorns, and torn by the Roman lance; a dying, agonizing human frame yielding up a disembodied human spirit. And let us measure by such a Death, demanded, exacted, endured, accomplished, the immensity of our need as sinners, and the immensity also of the reconciliation which is now for us—not to make, but to take. To Him be glory.

*REDEMPTION APPLIED: THE CASE OF
THE COLOSSIANS: THE APOSTLE'S
JOY AND AIM*

The grace that full salvation brings
  On me, e'en me, has shin'd;
The hope to which my spirit clings
  In Thee alone I find.

I look for Thee, for Thee I long,
  And Thy appearing bright,
When I shall join the heav'nly throng
  And shine in cloudless light.

HENRY MOULE, 1862.

## CHAPTER V

REDEMPTION APPLIED : THE CASE OF THE COLOS-
SIANS : THE APOSTLE'S JOY AND AIM

COLOSSIANS i. 21-29

WE all know the distinction in some fields of science between the "pure" and the "applied." Under the first is classed, for example, the study of figure and number in the abstract. Under the second, we think of the ways in which the principles so ascertained are used, for example in the construction of a bridge, or the measurement of a planet. In a certain sense we may carry the same distinction into religious thought. We may speak, with obvious reserves, of "pure" and 'applied" theology; the study of the facts of God and salvation as they are presented to us in themselves, and then the study of their action and effects as they are brought home with power to our human wills and lives.

Great and deep is the joy in every case of really "applied theology." It means the actual bringing together of God and man, the union of the sinner with his Saviour, present grace and future glory in the concrete instance of a being made "to glorify God and to enjoy Him fully for ever."

The great work of the minister of God's Word is to be the living and loving teacher of "applied theology." Let him spend his best and most prayerful pains upon learning the vital system "pure." Then let his life-work be to handle what he knows, in the presence and power of his Lord, so that it shall tell on "them that hear him" in its living "application."

The Apostle comes now to the theology of the glory and work of Christ—"applied" to the Colossians. Let us listen; for they were after all "our ensamples," τύποι ἡμῶν (1 Cor. x. 6), "types of us." In their fallen humanity we see ours; and their redemption shews us ours also.

As regards the grammar of the following passage, it will be necessary in our paraphrase to do it a slight violence. Grammatically, ver. 21 follows close upon 20 and 19; we must render, in strictness, somewhat thus: "The Father was pleased ... to reconcile to Himself all things ... on earth and in heaven, and (now particularly) *you*, who were alienated," etc. (ἀποκαταλλάξαι πάντα ... καὶ ὑμᾶς). Nevertheless it is legitimate to find here a pause of thought, although there is no break of construction. It seems clear that just at this point we do really pass from the general to the particular, with a view to the many detailed "applications" of the rest of the Epistle. I shall venture accordingly to treat ver. 21 as practically a new departure, and to render it as if it were worded somewhat thus: καὶ αὐτὸς ηὐδόκησε καὶ ὑμᾶς ἀποκαταλλάξαι, τούς ποτε ὄντας ἀπηλλοτριωμένους: "And He was pleased to reconcile you also, who were alienated once."

Ver. 21. **And you,** you among these "all things on earth," happy recipients in personal experience of this great mercy, you He was pleased to reconcile to Himself, in His gift of His Son for you and in His calling you into fellowship with Him by faith; **you, who once,** before a Saviour's coming, and before your coming to Him, **were estranged,** alienated, broken off from God in the Fall, **and enemies,** personally hostile (ἐχθρούς) to Him, the Eternal Holiness, **as to your thought,** your reasoning powers (διανοίᾳ), which approved and defended evil; **in your** (τοῖς) **works, your evil** works, the path "in" which your feet wandered. (But now, in the actual state of the case, in divine mercy—I cannot but pause, and throw in the glorious fact by the way—**you were reconciled**[1]; peace was made for you with

Ver. 22. God, **in the body of His flesh,** Christ's flesh, **by means of His death**[2]; "in" the blessed body of the Incarnate Lord of Calvary, because you were, in the mercy of God, taken as united to that Body, as if already mystically "its limbs"; and "by means of His *death*," because not Incarnation only but Propitiation was the awful requisite to your pardon.) Such is my glad passing thought about your actual reconciliation. Now let me return to the purpose and the issue of the Father's

---

[1] Read, probably, ἀποκατηλλάγητε. The sentence from νυνί to θανάτου is thus a parenthesis. On the meaning of "reconcile" see a note near the end of the chapter.

[2] Read, probably, τοῦ θανάτου αὐτοῦ.

"pleasure" in it: it was, **to present you** to Himself, **"in the day when He maketh up His jewels," holy, and without blemish, and without one accusation against you, before Himself**; for "who shall lay anything to your charge? It is Christ that died"; His merits secure your standing before the Judge; "such are you in the sight of God the Father as is the very Son of God Himself."[1] But that prospect is no reason for a faith indolent, unwatchful, fatalistic; "to your safety your sedulity is required"[2]; *from your side*, that prospect is only yours if, an emphatic "if" (εἴγε), **you are abiding by your** (τῇ) **faith**, holding fast to that great secret, simplest reliance on the all-sufficient Saviour, and on no substitute for Him; **founded** as on the Rock, **and steady** in the resolve to rest there for ever; **and not yielding to movements** (μετακινούμενοι, a present participle, indicating a chronic liability to disturbance) **away from the hope**, (the blessed hope of the Lord's Return for the final salvation of His waiting and faithful ones,) the **hope of the Gospel which you**

Ver. 23.

---

[1] Hooker, *Discourse of Justification*, ch. vi.—I take St Paul here to refer to the "righteousness of justification" rather than to the perfected personal holiness of the saints; having regard to Rom. viii. 33. But this latter thought, the prospect of their personal perfection as "Christ in them" is developed in the day of glory, lies very near at hand here.

[2] Again Hooker, *Sermon of the Perpetuity of Faith in the Elect*, at the end; a noble passage.

heard when you were first evangelized; **which was proclaimed**, when the Lord's *fiat* for it went out (Mark xvi. 15), **in all the creation which is under heaven**; among all our fellow-creatures without one limit of land or of tongue[1]; **of which Gospel I, Paul**, (individually named and designated to it by my Master, authentic in *my* commission, whoever claims without a warrant to be sent by Him,) **became**, was made, <u>a minister</u>, a working servant (διάκονος), when He called me to be His.

So he realizes anew, and recites to himself and to the Colossians, the unique greatness of the Gospel of the everlasting Son of the Father, that Gospel which had so blessed Colossæ, and which is also the One Gospel for the whole human world. And then he reaffirms his own high privilege, his call to be its authoritative steward and herald. "To him, less than the least of all the saints, is this grace given." And at once the joy

---

[1] For the hyperbole cp. Acts ii. 5; of the nations represented at Pentecost. Here however the reference is perhaps less to the actual than so to speak the ideal preaching of the Gospel—the preaching as it lay planned and purposed when the Lord commanded it. And in that respect the phrase "in all the creation under heaven" is not hyperbolical.

and the sufferings of apostolic labour rise upon his soul, and he proceeds:

Ver. 24. **Now,**[1] at this very hour, in this full, solemn view of Christ, His Gospel, your blessings received through it, its world-wide scope, and my great privilege in His commission, **now I am rejoicing in these** (τοῖς: omit μου) **sufferings on your behalf,** sufferings of unjust bonds and prison, necessitated by my labour and witness for you, as for all my converts; **and** I realize with gladness that **I am filling up, as required** (ἀντ-), with an endurance correspondent to the Master's and the work's demand, **what is lacking of the afflictions,**[2] the tribulation-toils, **of our** (τοῦ) **Christ,** toils begun by the Head, the supreme "Apostle of our profession," and left to

---

[1] "Who now"; A.V. But ὅς is certainly to be omitted.

[2] Θλίψεις: not παθήματα. He is thinking not of the Lord's Passion but of His sacred Life-work as Teacher, Healer, Guide, and meanwhile Endurer of "the contradiction of sinners." Lightfoot remarks that "the idea of expiation or satisfaction is wholly absent from this passage."—In the tribulations of His *Life*-work our blessed Lord, "though indeed pre-eminent, was not unique. He only '*began* to do and to teach' (Acts i. 1) personally what through His members He was to carry on to the end, and what was in this respect left incomplete when He quitted earth. Every true toiler and sufferer for Him and His flock contributes to the 'filling-up' of that incompleteness, so far as he toils and bears *in Christ*" (Note in the *Cambridge Bible*).

be completed by the members through whom He works; thus toiling **in my flesh**, in the willing use and exposure of my human faculties and energies, **on behalf of His body, which is the Church,**[1] inestimably dear to me for the sake of its glorious Head.

Ver. 25. **Of which Church, to serve its holy interests, I** (let me say it with a personal emphasis, ἐγώ, affirming my commission) **became**, at the Lord's call, **a minister** (διάκονος), **on the terms of** (κατά c. acc.), in a way conditioned by, **the stewardship of our** (τοῦ) **God, which was given me by Him with reference to you; to fulfil the word of God;** to develope His message till it is presented in its *fulness*[2]; that won-

Ver. 26. derful message, **the holy Secret** (μυστήριον[3]) **which had been kept hidden**, in the deep plan of God, **ever since the ages** (αἰῶνες) **and the generations** began; through all the cycles and developements of the history of intelligent creation, till the appointed hour; but **now** that hour has come, **now the Secret**

---

[1] See above, ver. 18.

[2] Cp. Rom. xv. 19: ὥστε με ... πεπληρωκέναι τὸ εὐαγγέλιον, "So that I have fully preached the Gospel" (A.V.).

[3] The word in N. T. always denotes a truth undiscoverable except by revelation, whether or no it is, when discovered, difficult or not to be understood.—The word is borrowed from the ancient systems of teaching and worship, whose rites of initiation were special and secret, and lay in a sense apart from and behind the popular religion.

has been manifested[1] to His saints, the men who have heard, believed, and yielded themselves to be Ver. 27. the Lord's; to whom God was pleased (for all was sovereign mercy, "according to His abundant mercy," "not according to our works," past, present, or to come) to make known, in His message, by His Spirit, what is the wealth of the glory, the treasures involved in the divine greatness and wonder, of this Secret in the Gentiles; as it is unfolded not only in Jewish but in once pagan hearts and lives, and draws them all into one Church of faith and love. And what is that Secret? It is not "it," but "He"; it is Christ in you, the hope of the coming glory; it is this Son of the Father's love, revealed as the Dweller in your beings, the Lord of your hearts, by faith; a Presence indissolubly connected with your eternal bliss, which will be but the full result of it. Even so the bud is "the hope" of the rose, the clear dawn is "the hope" of the summer day.

What shall we say over this long and not yet finished chain of truth, and joy, and most

---

[1] Ἐφανερώθη: the aorist refers to the historical facts of the Incarnation and Work of Christ, when "the grace of God which bringeth salvation appeared (ἐπεφάνη) for all men" (Tit. ii. 11). This is better expressed in English by the perfect, as an event comparatively recent and in its effects present.

blissful expectation? The heart of the Apostle in his prison is indeed "enlarged." It is as if nothing could be touched by him but it expands, dilating into depths and heights of grace and glory. He cannot speak of the "reconciliation" of the Colossians but he is lifted onward to the hour when they shall be presented without fault before the throne of God. He cannot speak of the faith of the Gospel, and of the urgent practical importance of their holding fast ($\dot{\epsilon}\pi\iota\mu\acute{\epsilon}\nu\epsilon\tau\epsilon$) by faith as their watchword, without going out and up to the fact that the Gospel of grace is the Lord's edict for the whole creation under heaven, for every human soul from the rising to the setting sun. He cannot speak of his apostolic labour but his heart burns with the thought that his toils and troubles are organically one with his beloved Lord's own ministry of word and work; that he is so profoundly one with Christ that his apostleship is but an extension of Him; that he is contributing to Christ's total of toil by laying out his own whole resources, in union with Him. He speaks of the Word of God, the message of salvation, and it shines before him as the Secret which lay hidden and hushed so long in the eternal Mind, but now has burst its long cloud, and pours its manifested sunshine on the saints. It is God's own disclosure, His answer to His own problem, meeting the whole need of man.

And now he cannot speak of that Secret but at once he unfolds it and translates it into nothing less than the personal Indwelling CHRIST. What is it? It is not an idea, a principle, a watchword. It is indeed the source and reason of all noble and powerful ideas, principles, and watchwords of salvation. But in itself, "IT is HE"; it is Jesus Christ. This Son of the Father's love, this Image of the invisible God, this Firstborn over all creation, and Head of the whole living Church—is Himself the "Secret." And this He is particularly in that wonderful aspect of Himself, His indwelling Presence.

Nothing less than this is His relation to His "saints." He makes reconciliation for them. He presides over them. He is their unifying Centre. But within all these operations, the innermost fact is this—He is in them. By

His Spirit, who unites the member and the Head, so that "he who is joined to the Lord is one spirit" (1 Cor. vi. 17), He is so present to all His own that nothing less than this word "in" satisfies the revealed thought.

In many a beautiful phrase He is presented to us in His wonderful proximity. "Come *unto* Me"; "The Lord is *near*"; "I am *with* you all the days"; "The Lord stood *with* me and strengthened me"; "To depart and to be *with* Christ"; "We shall ever be *with* the Lord"; "*Together with* Him." But these bright circles surround this yet more radiant centre; "Christ *in* you." So it is in that great Ephesian passage (iii. 14-17) which is unmistakably the developement of this briefer word: "I bow my knees unto the Father . . . that you may be strengthened with might by His Spirit, deep in (εἰς τόν) the inner man—that Christ may take up His abode in your hearts, by faith." So it is in the Lord's own wonderful promise (Rev. iii. 20) to the soul which has wandered but now listens and "looks again" in repentance and trust: "I will come *in to* him, and will sup with him, and he with Me."

Let us deal with this revealed blessing as with a fact of the covenant of God. It is not a thing for the arduous ambition of a few, who by difficult and heroic paths are to climb up to it. The indwelling of Christ in *the Christian* is presented to us as a normal, nay as a necessary, fact of all living Christianity; "Know ye not that Jesus Christ is in you, unless you are somehow (τι) counterfeits (ἀδόκιμοι)?" (2 Cor. xiii. 5). If we are in simplicity at His feet, He, thus indwelling by the Spirit, is in our being. And the indwelling "in *the heart*," what is it but this fact realized by the faith which sees and claims it? It is not an attainment; it is a recognition. "Come, and let us walk in the light of the Lord." Come, and let the Lord, humbly welcomed without misgiving, "dwell in us, and walk in us," every hour of life.

"The hope of glory." Such is the Apostle's description of the Indwelling, or rather of the Indweller, considered in one of the profound effects of His presence. What is "the reason of the hope that is in us" (1 Pet. iii. 15)? It is the Christ that is in us. He, recollected (and so, in measure, realized) as joined in the eternal life to our inmost being, He, welcomed not only into "us" in general but into our sanctuary, "the heart," is *ipso facto* the hope of glory; that glory which means our everlasting fruition of God in the heavenly state. Our expectation of that indescribable future is not as if we only "saw it afar off" and "embraced it," with wistful longings, across an intervening void. We are in vital contact with it already. "The hope of it" is HE who is the Lord of it. He is "the Lamb who is the lamp" of the eternal Jerusalem. And He is in us at this hour! To repeat our metaphors above; He is already in us as the bud of Himself the flower, the dawn of Himself the day.

> "Blessed are the sons of God;
> They are bought with Christ's own blood;
> One with God, with Jesus one,
> Glory is in them begun."

"Because I live"—and live in you—"ye shall live also," yes, with eternal life.

But a few verses yet claim attention before this section of our studies closes. He has named the Lord Christ; he pursues that Theme a step further still:

Ver. 28. **Whom**, as His own Gospel, **we**, emphatically we (ἡμεῖς), whatever be the message of other teachers, **proclaim**; carrying Him as our Tidings where we go; telling of Him as our Secret, alike for pardon and for holiness, for life and for law; **admonishing every man**, every individual, of his need of Christ and his allegiance to Christ, **and instructing every man in all wisdom**, in all applications of that holy wisdom which means the right living of a life of faith and love; (for the will of God is that *every* disciple should learn *every* duty of consistent holiness;) **in order that we may present** to the Lord, when He returns and His servants come to meet Him, "bringing their sheaves with them," **every man**, thus taught how to use his wealth of grace, **perfect**, mature, developed, no longer the babe and beginner[1] but the adult, **in Christ**,[2] in his union with his Head, who is to every "limb" the true cause and law of

---

[1] Τέλειον. Lightfoot thinks that this is a term borrowed from the "mysteries." But it seems sufficient and appropriate to render it as above.

[2] Omit Ἰησοῦ.

its full developement. Such is our aim; nothing less than the entire personal holiness, in union and communion with Christ, of every human being whom we have led to Him. It is the will of God that it should be so. And the whole power of His Son is with and in His disciples, that it may be so. Therefore for me (I speak for myself) that goal, impossible for man, is possible, attainable, infinitely to be desired: **towards which** end **I am actually** (καί) **toiling** to my uttermost (κοπιῶ), like the racer towards his point of victory, **striving**, like him as he contends with fatigue and faintness in the arena, **according to**, with a hope and a renewal of strength conditioned by, **His**, my Master's, **active force** (ἐνέργειαν); that force **which is acting in me in power**. For indeed in me, by His mercy, the Christ whom I preach is present, not as hope of glory only but as power for service. "By Him I move, and in Him live." And the toil, however it may exhaust the bodily nature, is in Him lifted above exhaustion for the spirit. "I run, and am not weary, I walk, and do not faint," because of Him.

[marginal note: Ver. 29.]

The messages of these few lines are weighty.

i. Let us note first, what has already so often come up in the apostolic teaching, the identification of the Gospel with its Lord. He is His Gospel. "WHOM we preach" is the phrase, when St Paul is about to say how he is labouring to edify his converts. His inexhaustible longing is that they may live a full Christian life; cautioned, instructed, growing, mature. He has much to say to them about the methods; but the much is all summed up in the One—"WHOM we preach." Christ in His Person, in His reconciliation, in His indwelling life, in His coming glory, HE is the secret of the Christian alike for the beginnings and for the last developements of his regenerate condition and its activities.

These Colossian disciples, like all disciples everywhere and in every age, "began fallen"; "began life with the face away from God." They were "alienated," "personal enemies" of the Holy One, potentially and then actually. They were what he describes them as being in the expanded parallel passage in Ephesians (ch. ii. 1-3, 11, 12); "dead in their trespasses and their sins; by nature children of wrath; sundered from ($\chi\omega\rho\iota\varsigma$) Christ, alienated from the commonwealth of the (true) Israel, strangers to the covenants of the promise; feeling no hope (ἐλπίδα μὴ ἔχοντες), and without God in the world." To all this there is applied the antidote of JESUS CHRIST; and it is adequate. To HIM they were led by grace through the Gospel. In Him the dead found life, the condemned found reconciliation, that is to say, the more than amnesty of the injured KING, His glad while righteous welcome of them back,[1] in the atoning, dying, Son. In Him the alienated found a wonderful instatement. They were incorporated indeed into "the

---

[1] "Reconciliation" in Scripture is a word which habitually denotes the gracious concessions of an offended personage, welcoming the offender back. The offender thus "is reconciled" in respect not of *his* laying aside resentment and consenting to obey, but in respect of the other party laying aside *his* resentment, and consenting to receive. See e.g 1 Sam. xxix. 4; "Wherewith should he (David) reconcile himself unto his (offended) master? Should it not be even with the heads of these men?" In the light of such an example of usage cp. 2 Cor. v. 20, "Be ye reconciled to God"; *i.e.* seek and secure, in the atonement (ver. 21) of His Son, His gracious amnesty and welcome.—This will justify the scriptural *meaning* of the apparently opposite *phraseology* of Art. ii., on the Atonement; "That He might reconcile His Father to us"; words which convey the same thought, but with a use of "reconcile" such as we are more accustomed to. And for this use (and the scriptural fitness therefore of the phrase in the Article) cp. Luke xviii. 13, "O God, *be reconciled* (ἱλάσθητι, be propitiated) to me the sinner."

commonwealth of Israel," for they were incorporated into its living King! In Him the hopeless, the beings conscious of no faintest approach to a genuine hope beyond the tomb, (how eloquent is the witness of the whole elegiac literature of the classics to this!) found "the hope of glory" which was revealed in their risen Saviour; and His presence in their very being was the guarantee that it was not a dream. And now in their profound experience of moral weakness and pollution this same Jesus Christ is, according to St Paul, the answer and the resource still. In view of the question, how can we stand, and grow, and be adult spiritual men, He is the secret. He must stand in them, and they will stand. HE must grow in them, and they will grow, growing up, on *their* side, "into Him" (Eph. iv. 15). He must abide in them, and they in Him, and they shall ripen into the holy adultness of purity, and truthfulness, and love.

"Our sacred books in the East contain many noble precepts. Your sacred Book contains not only the precepts, but the secret how to do them." So said a young Japanese student to me at Cambridge, many years ago, on the eve of a wonderful discovery of the glory of Christ. It is even thus. The "secret how to do" *is* in our sacred Book; and it is— "CHRIST in you; WHOM we preach."

ii. Then let us not fail to note the Apostle's restless longing for just this; that the "precepts" *should*, in the power of this "secret," be "done." He has won these Colossian souls to faith; he sees them lodged in Christ, redeemed, reconciled, filled with the hope of glory. But therefore he is insatiably desirous that they should be *taught* (διδάσκοντες) the depth and range of Christian holiness, and should be *cautioned* (νουθετοῦντες) against every inconsistency, and should so grow that when the Lord comes they may be presented (παραστήσωμεν) before Him not as stunted products of redemption, but as the mature and developed (τέλειον) sons of God. And this is his longing not for a few, for an inner circle, for such as might elect to follow "counsels of perfection" while the rest might be allowed to walk contentedly on a lower level. He is spending his soul upon the effort to get this holiness developed in "every man," "every man," "every man"; the words recur again and again with urgent emphasis. It may be, as Lightfoot thinks, that he is here contrasting his aim with that of the Gnostic teacher, who avowedly aimed at the illumination (so he thought it to be) of only an esoteric circle. But anywise this *is* St Paul's urgent, we may almost say passionate, aim—the unreserved and instructed obedience, the adult holiness, of every individual, man and woman (ἄνθρωπον), that has come to Christ. In this sense, to him, there is no esoteric circle; or rather, the whole circle is esoteric. Must it not be so, when the feeblest "member" is "in" the Head; when the being once alienated, whoever he may be, now has "Christ in him, the hope of glory"?

iii. Lastly, the Missionary's toil for this edification (not merely evangelization) of the Colossians is exhausting; yet he is not exhausted. He "toils" (κοπιῶ), not only works; yet he does not faint. And why? Because the secret he proclaims for others is his own. Christ is in him, working in him, working with power. To Christ he yields himself as instrument, as vehicle; and so nothing less than Christ's energy is what he has to spend upon the blessed toil.

# THE SECRET OF GOD, AND ITS POWER

THE Sun of Righteousness on me
　　Hath rose, with healing in His wings;
Wither'd my nature's strength, from Thee
　　My soul its life and succour brings;
My help is all laid up above,
Thy nature and Thy name is Love.

　　　　　　　　　　　C. WESLEY.

# CHAPTER VI

### THE SECRET OF GOD, AND ITS POWER

#### COLOSSIANS ii. 1-7

"STRIVING, according to His active force, which is acting within me in power." Such has been St Paul's last word (i. 29) about his life and labour for his converts. His phraseology, as so often, is full of the Greek *palæstra* with its wrestlers, and of the Greek *stadium* with its races. The persistent grapple with opposing limbs, the toiling energies all bent upon the goal and the victorious wreath; these scenes are in his mind, and shape his thought, and point his words. He is conscious of a power not his own "acting within him," a reserve of force inexhaustible, with which to wrestle and to run. But he is equally aware that for him, as truly as for any competitor who ever entered the Corinthian or the Olympian lists, it was necessary *to use* the power within him. The Lord is in him; He is His servant's "arm every morning" (Isa. xxxiii. 2). But he, in the Lord's Name, must use the Arm, for labour and for strife. The powers which wrestle with him for the ruin of his work are real, and are resolute; he must indeed meet them, foot to foot, force to force, in Christ. His enemy would do anything to divert his gaze from the goal, and to make his foot slip as he goes; he means nothing less than Paul's total failure. Then Paul, having God working in him, must "run, not uncertainly"; he must put out freely the resources of the indwelling Life.

But now, what *is* the contest? Is it, just at present, some great enterprise of external labour? Is it to attack another continent for Christ? To brave new shipwrecks, and new riots, on the way from shore to shore, or town to town, proclaiming the blessed Name? Not at all. Such "striving" is at present physically impossible for him. The whole travelling activity of the Apostle is limited now by the walls, doors, and bolts of "the hired lodging," and by the chain which attaches him to the Prætorian sentinel. Whatever he does, whatever he endures or achieves, he must now do it—sitting still. Yes, but he can "strive according to the active force" of his Lord none the less powerfully and effectually for this. It is more than ever open to him in this compulsory retirement to wrestle and to run in intercessory PRAYER.

Prayer is now his grave and assiduous occupation; his toil, his course. The opening words of ch. ii., the passage at present before us, tell us this. He is working hard, like the wrestler on the ribbed floor of the Olympian court; he is engaged in a long indefatigable effort for the Colossian converts, and their neighbours. And it all means—Prayer.

Whole treatises have been written on the Prayers of St Paul. Those prayers afford rich material for exposition, as they lie scattered over the Epistles, and let us into the depths of this wonderful man's heart, and, through that heart and its desires, give us fresh sights of Christ's grace and glory. One of those prayers we have already gone over in these chapters. But let us pause here a little while to consider not so much the matter of St Paul's prayers as, so to speak, their manner. As we read them, for example in this Epistle, or in Ephesians, or more briefly in Philippians, we read a series of well-ordered utterances, all pregnant with the living truths of revelation. We can, if we please, study them from a purely doctrinal standpoint; so full and rich is their language about grace, and glory, and holiness, and Christ. But what was *the manner* of these prayers, not as they are recorded but as they were uttered? It was the manner of a conflict (ἀγών); it was a wrestle.

I cannot doubt that this meant often an importunity which expressed itself in urgent visible action. It must have made the Prætorian wonder to see this extraordinary prisoner at his prayers; to watch his agitation of look and bearing, to hear his voice labouring to utter all his heart, in tones half suppressed sometimes, but sometimes not suppressed at all; to mark the falling tears, or the kindling smiles, as the direction of the supplication changed. May we not be sure that it was often so? And would not these scenes often be *prolonged*? If St Paul's metaphor of the wrestle is true to itself, the prayer would be no brief crisis of devotion. It would go on, and on. It would be like those almost interminable strifes in the Greek games, of which the antiquarians tell us, when the "pancratiasts" would try strength and skill against one another far on from the day into the night. To take an illustration infinitely more noble, it would be as when in the ravine of Jabbok the Patriarch wrestled with the mysterious Man, and persevered with Him till the day broke over the dark eastern hill.

Nothing is more likely than that St Paul thus openly strove with God in prayer, in the room where he was never alone for one minute. We must remember that he was an Oriental, and that Oriental gravity is somehow strangely exempt from our Western shyness in matters of religion. I have myself seen, in a railway carriage, between Jerusalem and Jaffa, a Moslem, a prominent official of the port, before the whole company in the saloon-car, draw off his shoes, gather up his feet, and address himself to a long half-hour of audible prayer; totally indifferent, so he seemed, to all around him while he recited the Names of Alláh, and deliberately chanted his ascription and adoration. We must remember the Oriental in the Apostle, and also that the sentinel at his side, though probably not an Asiatic, was probably a *southern* European. Far less, very far less, than with us would one of these men ·in the presence of the other shrink from unreserved and prolonged devotion.

But this after all is a mere accessory. The heart of the fact before us is not the outward but the inward "manner" of St Paul's prayers for his converts. It was the manner of a wrestle of the soul. Visible or not to human eyes, it was this to his Lord; a sustained, importunate, courageous conflict; a strife with all and anything which would withstand his praying, and with all and anything which would suggest to him that his Lord was not listening, and would not bless.

This double aspect of the effort we trace in the word " conflict." He sets himself to pray, and he meets with obstacles to the act of prayer ; perhaps bodily weariness, or pain, or the importunity of other thoughts. He wrestles with these things ; he is not to be overcome ; he " stirs himself up to lay hold on God"; it shall be no light thing that keeps him back from a real "access with confidence." And then *in* the work of praying, once well begun, he is tempted to misgive. The Lord *seems* to "answer never a word "; or to answer only with the apparent negative of new anxieties and disappointments about the beloved converts for whom he strives. " Is not the effort vain, visionary, misdirected ? Is not your God unfavourable or at best passive in this matter over which your heart is working so hard ? Are you quite sure that He hears ? Does the Infinite really attend to you ? Can the fact of your longings and their verbal utterance affect the Absolute ? Are you not pouring the prayer, not into an ear which listens, and so into a heart which loves, but into the fathomless void ?" And then with these enemies also he wrestles. He recalls the hope that is in him. He recollects his Lord, and he thrusts the obstacles aside, and prays on. "He will not let HIM go."

Prayer is indeed a many-sided thing. True prayer can be uttered under innumerably different conditions. Often, very often,

> "Prayer is the burthen of a sigh,
> The falling of a tear,
> The upward glancing of an eye,
> When none but God is near."

Prayer, genuine and victorious, is continually offered without the least physical effort or disturbance. It is often in the deepest stillness of soul and body that it wins its longest way. But there is another side of the matter. Prayer is never meant to be *indolently* easy, however simple and reliant it may be. It is meant to be an infinitely important transaction between man and God. And therefore very often, when subjects and circumstances call for it, it has to be viewed as a work involving labour, persistency, conflict, if it would be prayer indeed.

A visitor knocked betimes one morning at

the door of a good man, a saint of the noblest Puritan type; and that was a fine type indeed. He called as a friend to consult a friend, sure of his welcome. But he was kept waiting long; at last a servant came to explain the delay; "My master has been at prayer, and this morning he has been long in getting access."

Such anecdotes are not meant to "bring us into bondage," as if because this was once the case with one loyal servant of God we are unfaithful servants if our prayers are sometimes easy, and ready, and comparatively brief. Nor are St Paul's "conflicts" to be quoted for such an inference either. But the records of toil and strife in prayer have a message nevertheless for all believers. They remind us that prayer, if true, is a transaction worth taking laborious pains about, if we find this needful in order to "get access." The fatal danger is, to be content without "getting access," and so only to play with prayer.

But now let us listen to this man, just come from his wrestle before God.

Ver. 1. **For I wish you to know,** so that your

sympathies may go with my petitions for you, how severe (ἡλίκον) a conflict I am having, against all that withstands my intercessions, on behalf of (ὑπέρ : so read) you, and the converts in Laodicea,[1] and all who have never seen my face in flesh.[2] For you, and for them, I have been indeed wrestling in prayer, under a profound impression of their dangers and their needs;

Ver. 2. that their hearts, their thoughts, affections, wills, **may be encouraged** (παρακληθῶσιν); they being (read συμβιβασθέντες) knit together, compacted, welded into genuine unity, **in love**, and so enabled to rise **to the whole wealth** (εἰς πᾶν τὸ πλοῦτος) **of the full exercise of their** (τῆς) **intelligence,**

---

[1] An important town about eleven miles from Colossæ, to the west, in the same river-valley. It is nothing now but a vast scene of ruins.—Cp. iv. 13, 15, 16, and Rev. iii. 14, for mentions of Laodicea.—In 363 a small Council was held at Laodicea, where for the first time the question was officially put, what sacred Books should be considered canonical and inspired, to the exclusion of all others.

[2] Grammatically, this clause may or *may not* mean that the Colossians and Laodiceans had never seen St Paul. But common sense seems to decide for its meaning that they had not seen him. It is difficult otherwise to see the point of him *naming* Colossæ and Laodicea specially and alone, whilst the language is natural if they were the leading instances of Churches closely connected with him but which he had never personally visited. For them, and for such as them, he would thus feel a *distinctive* anxiety, having so much to do with them, yet never having had the opportunity of fully and orally instructing and warning them.

resulting in (εἰς) the true (ἐπι-) knowledge of the mystery of God, the Secret He has to disclose for

Ver. 3. our full felicity—even Christ[1]; in whom are all the treasures of His (τῆς) wisdom and His knowledge, hidden there. HE is the Father's glorious Casket, in which are shut all the mysteries and treasures of grace, planned and wrought by the eternal Mind, and so "hidden" in Him that, outside Him, "eye hath not seen them, nor have they entered into the heart of man to conceive"; aye, and even in Him they are hidden still, veiled in their own glory, as to our *completed* knowledge.

Ver. 4. **Now this I say**—this word about my importunate prayer that you may all grow, and grow together with one another, in the knowledge of Christ's hidden glory—**in order that no one may reason you over with** (ἐν) **beguiling talk**, persuading you to think another path to peace and holiness more safe, more reasonable, more honourable, than

---

[1] A maze of various readings meets us here. The two most important are τοῦ μυστηρίου τοῦ Θεοῦ πατρὸς Χριστοῦ, and τοῦ μ. τοῦ Θεοῦ Χριστοῦ. This latter phrase grammatically may mean either, "of the mystery of *our* (τοῦ) *God Christ*"; or, "of the mystery of *the God of Christ*"; or, "of the mystery *of our God* (*which mystery is*) *Christ.*" But the parallel words of i. 27, τοῦ μυστηρίου, ὅς ἐστι Χριστός, are strongly in favour of the last rendering.—The *reading* adopted by us here is advocated elaborately by Bp Lightfoot, and preferred on the whole by Dr Scrivener.

this one Way of Christ. Is the anxiety needless? No; for, far away as I am, I yet seem to *see* your present happy state, and can only dread the more acutely the dangers which already threaten it.

Ver. 5. **For though** (εἰ) **actually** (καί) **as to my** (τῇ) **flesh I am absent, yet as to my** (τῷ) **spirit I am with you, rejoicing over you, and looking at your order,** your orderly array (τάξιν), as that of the Lord's disciplined soldiers, **and at the solidity,** the solid front,[1] **of your faith in Christ,** your spiritual coherence and steadfastness, due to your common reliance on your Lord.[2] But if such is, as it is, your present happy state, see that it is continued, in a continuous dependence on the same glorious Secret.

Ver. 6. **Therefore, as you received the Christ,** even **Jesus, the Lord,** the one blessed historic Jesus, Theme of prophets, King of your souls; no mystic dream of speculation on the one hand, no mere human teacher and exemplar on the other, but Son of Man, Christ of God; so, even so, according to that once-welcomed, unalterable Truth, **in Him walk;** live your whole life in genuine union with Him;

Ver. 7. **having taken root** (ἐρριζωμένοι, perfect), and

---

[1] "Orderly array" and "solid front" are Lightfoot's renderings for τάξιν and στερέωμα.

[2] With the words στερέωμα τῆς πίστεως compare Acts xvi. 5, αἱ ἐκκλησίαι ἐστερεοῦντο τῇ πίστει, and 1 Pet. v. 9, ᾧ ἀντίστητε, στερεοὶ τῇ πίστει.

now getting builded up (ἐποικοδομούμενοι, present), in Him (as He is at once the deep genial soil of your life and growth and the corner-stone of your ascending structure); **and getting stablishment** (βεβαιούμενοι: note the present participle) **by your faith** (τῇ πίστει), **just as you were taught,** (for the old truth is the eternal truth;) **abounding in it,** in your faith, in the glad exercise of it as you go, **in thanksgiving.** For the more you believe, the more you will be constrained to give thanks. And to live a life of thanksgiving is a deep secret for soundness and persistency in the truth of the Gospel.

That last word, "with thanksgiving," is surely no mere rhetorical cadence to a paragraph. It conveys what I have briefly indicated in closing the paraphrase once more, a deep and beautiful precept for the Christian life. Do you believe in Christ? And do you live amidst surroundings unfavourable to your faith? Is it directly assailed? Is it secretly undermined? Are you shocked by crude denials? Are you bewildered, made wistful, half saddened, half allured, by speculative substitutes for the Gospel of the Cross, the New Birth, the Fulness of the Spirit, the blessed Hope?

Use all lawful means of mental and spiritual resistance. "Gird up the loins of your *mind*" (1 Pet. i. 13). Recall the vast "reason of the hope that is in you," so that you do it "with meekness and fear" (1 Pet. iii. 15). But among other preservatives, do not forget this; "in your faith, abound in thanksgiving." There is a great and profoundly reasonable power in holy thanksgiving to bring home to the soul the reality of the Treasure for which the thanks are given. The heart which looks up and blesses God for "His unspeakable Gift," His own Son, "who was delivered for our offences, raised for our justification," and glorified for our life and glory, will develope a holy and healthy instinct of rejection towards all substitutes for Him. Just so to the Philippians (iii. 1) St Paul writes, "Rejoice in the Lord," because he is so sure, amidst the spiritual dangers he sees around them, that to rejoice in the Lord "for them *is safe*."

Let classical legend for once contribute its comment and illustration to divine truth. "The Sirens, by the sweetness of their magic songs, decoyed upon the rocks the mariners who sailed past their isles, and the shores were white with human bones. Ulysses with his crew, and Orpheus, by different means escaped the danger. Ulysses stopped the ears of his men with wax, and (wishing himself to hear the song, and to hear it in safety) caused himself to be fast bound to the mast. Orpheus took another method; he raised his voice to the harp in loud and long praises of the immortal Gods, and thus overcame the charm of the Sirens with another and a better charm. 'Far the best in every way,' says Bacon,[1] 'is the remedy of Orpheus; for meditations upon things divine surpass the delights of sense not in power only but in sweetness also.'"[2]

No heart is more vulnerable to doubt and to spiritual delusion than the unthankful heart, which will not walk in the sunshine of the Lord. No fence, many a time, proves stronger against the melancholy Sirens of misbelief than the heart which says (and the heart *can*

---

[1] *Wisdom of the Ancients.*
[2] From a note to a Poem by the author; *The Beloved Disciple.*

say) to itself, "My meditation of Him shall be sweet; *I will* be glad in the Lord."

But then, such gladness, such thanksgiving, must ever be feeding and living not upon itself but upon its Cause, its Secret. We must go off and up to Him for the renewal and permanence of thanksgiving. We must "consider Him." And, "as we have received Him," through the message of His Word, made vital by His Spirit, "so we must walk in Him" in common life. We must recollect Him as Root. We must use Him as Stone of foundation, and Stone of the corner. Thus we shall abound, as in faith, so in thanksgiving.

This is just the point of the whole Epistle, as we have repeatedly seen. The most dangerous travesties of the Gospel were penetrating the quiet circles of Colossæ. St Paul meets them not with a restatement of abstract principles, but with the incessant presentation of Jesus Christ. And now, particularly, he has presented to us the Lord Jesus in just this character—the Secret of God. As we close, let us pause a little in thought before that word.

Great is the charm of secrecy, of the mysterious. The "mysteries" of old Greece drew innumerable minds with an almost supernatural magnet, to seek initiation. The cause must have lain in part in the noble purity and elevation, at least by comparison, of the teachings of Eleusis. But a powerful concurrent cause surely was the charm of secrecy. In our own day, who, of the uninitiated, has not at one time or another felt the attraction of the occultness of Freemasonry? This instinct was largely present in the early perversions or counterfeits of the Gospel of the grace of God; it was evidently thus with "the Colossian heresy." Whatever the alien teachers taught, they gave it out that they possessed a secret, and invited candidates for initiation, who should in their turn keep the secret from all uninitiated minds. The Apostle meets them on their own ground; he has a Secret too. It is unknown, it is unknowable, save to the initiated soul. It can be looked at from outside by any one, as any one could enter the outer courts of the great Attic sanctuary of Demeter, and look at that inner temple where the mystics went in alone. But no one could know this blessed Secret without entrance in. JESUS CHRIST—any one could read the syllables, who knew the alphabet. Any one could learn the facts of the history. Any one, possessed of a mind, could apprehend the proof of them as facts, the Resurrection from the garden-tomb included. Yet Christ remained a Secret, till man had come to Him, and had asked to enter in, and had entered in, believing. Then He was revealed. Seen from within, He shone from all sides upon the wondering sinner's soul, the Secret of God—disclosed. He proved Himself then the Answer of the Eternal to the questions of the agonized conscience, of the weary heart, of the broken will, of the man "who through fear of death was all his lifetime subject to bondage." "I know whom I have believed."

"Nought from them is hidden, knowing Him to whom all things are known."[1]

---

[1] From the hymn of Petrus Damianus (cent. xi.) *de Gaudiis Paradisi*, in Trench's *Sacred Latin Poetry*.

Yet even thus, wonderful and delightful fact, though He is revealed, He is still the Secret. "The treasures" are still in Him "*hidden*," "*hiddenly*" (ver. 3), as one expositor has rendered it. For though He has been found, yet He, this same Jesus, is the Almighty; and "canst thou find out the Almighty unto perfection?" (Job xi. 7). The happy believer has found the treasure-house; but it is a labyrinth; its riches are unsearchable. *For ever*, though he knows his Lord as the world does not and cannot know Him, he will never know the riches that are hid in Him; he will never touch the depth; he will never issue out upon the other side.

Happy and holy initiation, in that divine Eleusis! And let the privileged votaries, within the Temple, often hold mutual converse about the wonders they are given to see; even as St Paul prayed that the Colossians might be "knit *together in love*" that they might all the better "*know* the wealth of the Secret."

And then let them often go to the Temple

door and, remembering the will of God, cry aloud in the accents of certainty and joy, " Him that cometh unto Jesus Christ, He will in no wise cast out."

*PARDON, LIFE, AND VICTORY IN THE
CRUCIFIED AND RISEN ONE*

Jésus-Christ est le Dieu de l'homme, comme l'a si bien dit Pascal dans quelques pages où il développe d'une manière profondément chrétienne la place que Jésus-Christ occupe entre Dieu et nous. Il est le Dieu de l'homme; il est Dieu qui s'est donné à nous; il s'est donné tout entier; et quand nous possédons Jésus-Christ par une foi véritable, nous ne possédons rien moins que Dieu lui-même, et en lui la vie éternelle.

Ad. Monod, *Adieux*.

# CHAPTER VII

PARDON, LIFE, AND VICTORY IN THE CRUCIFIED AND RISEN ONE

Colossians ii. 8–15

"CHRIST, the Secret of God"; this was the watchword of the paragraph traversed in our last chapter. The same supreme topic rises before us in that which we now approach. We shall find everywhere this same wonderful Christ, the divine Antithesis to error and to evil. He is here before us, the antidote to a false philosophy. He is literally the *embodiment* of the Fulness of the Godhead, and we, in Him, derive that Fulness into our needing souls. He is the vital Head of all power, and of all Powers. He is the Minister of the true circumcision of the Spirit. In Him, and in Him alone, man finds his inward resurrection to new life. In Him, the Lord of the better Covenant, is laid up for us, and is given to us, a perfect pardon, won through the Cross. He, on that Cross, achieved overwhelming and eternal victory over the dark personal powers of evil, His enemies and ours. Would we have peace? Would we have purity? Would we have inexhaustible resource for life and holiness? Would we have strength for victory, triumphing over the devil, the world, and the flesh? The answer is still the same. Christ is the Secret of God.

Perhaps no passage even in this Epistle calls for closer attention to its phrase and argument than does this. Here and there it presents us with some of those spiritual stars of the first magnitude which have always arrested the attention of the Christian. But everywhere this field is "sown thick with stars"; and we have need of special watchfulness and observation. We approach our paraphrase in that spirit. We will work in a somewhat piecemeal fashion, pausing occasionally for fuller notice by the way.

Ver. 8. **Take care lest any one**[1] (for such persons there are, known to me, but not named) **be your spoiler,** your captor, leading you off as his helpless prey into the land of error, **by means of his empty delusion of a philosophy,**[2] his alleged system and theory of truth and life, **according to,** on the line and scale of, **the tradition**[3] **of men,** the teaching "handed on" in secrecy and mystery from one dreamer to another, and wholly human in its origin all the while; **according to the elements of the world,** the elementary lessons[4] of rite and ordinance which the Gospel has superseded, and which now, if put

---

[1] Lightfoot points out that this expression is often used by St Paul when he alludes to opponents whom he does not care to specify. Cp. 1 Cor. xi. 16, xv. 12; 2 Cor. iii. 1, x. 2, 12, xi. 20, 21; Gal. i. 7, 9; 2 Thess. iii. 10, 11; 1 Tim. i. 3, 6, vi. 3, 21.

[2] Lit., "by the (his) philosophy and empty delusion." The second term explains and exposes the first; and our paraphrase will fairly represent this.

[3] Παράδοσις, "tradition," may, and often does, mean merely "teaching," without any thought of secrecy, or any distinction from the common revealed truth. Cp. 2 Thess. ii. 15, iii. 6. In this sense παράδοσις and *traditio* are frequently used, by the Greek and Latin Fathers respectively, for *Holy Scripture itself.*—Strictly, "tradition" means "what is handed on" to us, whether orally or in writing. But here obviously it bears a more occult sense; an alleged secret transmission of mysteries.

[4] Στοιχεῖα: so Gal. iv. 3. The word means first a simple "element," e.g. a sound going to make up a word. Then an element or early principle in teaching; so no doubt here.

into competition with the Gospel, are of "the world," non-spiritual, **and not according to Christ.**

We reach the sacred watchword here, and pause to listen to it. Οὐ κατὰ Χριστόν, "not *according to Christ*"; not on His line, not measured by Him, not referred to Him; not so that He is Origin, and Way, and End, and All. The "philosophy" in question would assuredly include Him somehow in its terms. But it would not be "according to Him." It would take its principles, and draw its inferences, *à priori* and from other regions; and then bring Him in as something to be harmonized and assimilated, as far as might be. But this would mean a Christ according to the system of thought, not a system of thought according to the blessed Christ. And for St Paul the one true system of spiritual thinking must be altogether "according to" Him. It must have Him for Alpha, and for

---

Then a "heavenly body," regarded as a first ground in time-measurement; and some ancient expositors see this here, as if St Paul had been referring to "seasons and times" of ritual observance; new moons, etc. But this is far-fetched.

Omega, and for all the alphabet between. It must be dominated all over by Him. It must "know nothing" as its burthen, as its wisdom, as its aim and ambition in research, but Him.

This would mean no dwarfed or withered state of the Christian intellect; rather the very opposite. The thinking power, working on and on "according to Christ," would find no lack of depth and height, length and breadth, to expatiate in. Let a man of elevated and penetrating understanding get a true view of the Christ of God, as the Word shews Him and the Spirit glorifies Him, and he will have a subject-matter for his whole mental powers such as he never had before. But the very law of his thought now, its guarantee at once for freedom and for security, will be to think "according to Christ." He will find himself now not studying Christ in the light of other things, but studying everything else in the light of Christ. Christ will no longer be a light, however brilliant, shining among others in the firmament of thought. He will be the Sun of the sky. He will be the Sun of the whole rolling system.

Well may He be so, when we ponder the words in which St Paul now sets forth His glory.

Ver. 9. **For in Him resides,** as in a settled and congenial home (κατοικεῖ), **all the fulness of the Deity**[1] (θεότητος), the whole glorious total of what God is, the supreme Nature in its infinite entirety[2]; **in bodily fashion,** conditioned now as to its manifestation and communication by His sacred bodily state. It is in Him not only as He is the SON, but as He is the Son INCARNATE. It is not *limited and confined* by the fact that "He became flesh and tabernacled in us." But it is brought unspeakably *near to us* by that fact, made as it were gloriously tangible and accessible to us His human brethren, to whom this wonderful Bearer of the divine Fulness is now joined as Man. Yes, He is joined to us, and we to Him; He is in us, and we in Him. And thus this Fulness is for us, His members. We are in Him; and It is in Him. So we are as it were immersed in It, and filled with It, as a vessel dipped in the sea is filled with the very sea itself.

---

[1] The Latin word *Deitas* was coined in Christian times, apparently on purpose to render Θεότης more fully than the vaguer *Divinitas*.

[2] See above, on ch. i. 19.

Ver. 10. **And you are** (emphatically so, not "you may be" but "you *are*") **in Him filled full** of the Fulness; in His promise, presence, power, you do possess "*all things* needful for life and godliness." Just so far as you rely upon Him and draw upon Him, you "possess your possessions," you realize your wealth, you are filled in fruition with what already fills you in potency. United thus to Him, and filled thus in Him, what need have you to go to a lower range of spiritual forces for peace and holiness? **For He** (ὅς) **is the Head of every government and authority**; all the ranks and orders of the Unseen, how glorious soever, are but limbs of Him their Head. And you are His limbs too, and He is your Head, in the wonder of His living union with you. Live then, for it is your right and it is your life to do so, live at and on the Fountain itself; nothing but Christ, nothing between.

It is the truth which meets us everywhere in the revelation of Christ in His Word; "nothing between." The weakest and most unworthy believer is here seen as "joined unto the Lord" with an immediateness quite absolute. Not by the intervention of the Church, as if through it he must reach Christ, and touch Him, and live by Him. Not by the intervention of other mediators, the supposed members of a pantheon of unseen powers, angelic and human, carrying up to the throne the distant echo of our faith, and bringing back through long channels something of the life divine. No; it is a far nearer, far simpler, but also far more wonderful matter. "He that is joined unto the Lord is one spirit" (1 Cor. vi. 17). The "limb," in this mystical body, is articulated always direct into the Head. The man is articulated into all other living limbs; but through the Head. He is in them through Christ, not in Christ through them. He is in this respect as near to the Lord as not only any other believer, and as all believers taken together, but as "angels, and archangels, and all the company of heaven." "Let him love, and sing, and wonder." Let him also use to the utmost, now and here, his blessed position—"filled full in Him in whom resides all the Fulness," and "who is the Head of all government and authority," being also the Head, equally, of the believing sinner in his need.

The Apostle now goes on to speak of this

union in respect of its beginning. How did they enter on it? From one point of view, in the outward order, by their Baptism. From another point of view, in the inward order, by their Faith. The relation did not exist once; it was no necessary fact in the past. They were once "outside Christ" (χωρὶς Χριστοῦ, Eph. ii. 12). They were not at all "in Him," and so indeed they were not "filled full in Him." But divine mercy had prepared a way of entrance, into covenant, into life, into pardon, and peace, and holiness, and heaven, because into Christ. That way was the glorious counterpart to the circumcision of the old Israel, in which was given both a symbolical separation from pollution and a definite ceremonial institution into blessing. The way of entrance was from one side Baptism, from the other side Faith; faith, the sinner's acceptance of the divine terms and grant; baptism, the divine seal upon the grant and the acceptance. Baptism, so viewed, not as the substitute for faith but as the seal upon the promise, and upon the validity of our acceptance of it, is spoken of " in terms of the thing it signifies." And so it is described as the spiritual burial and resurrection of the man, and as his gate of entrance into an abundant and assured pardon, and into the very victory won by his crucified Lord over the whole universe of evil.

Let us keep these principles in view as we go on to the passage before us. They are sure principles of the Gospel, above all, as it is unfolded by St Paul. Union with Christ is the very life of our spirits. In union with Christ we possess all His treasures. We possess the "forgiveness of all our trespasses," in the sense of peace with God as His adopted and accepted children. We read our condemnation cancelled, as it hangs on the Lord's Cross, fastened there, and torn there, by the ensanguined nails. We possess a divine separation from sin's polluting grasp and claim. We possess a resurrection-life, holy, endless, in our risen Redeemer. And how do we enter upon it all? By "the circumcision of Christ"; the circumcision, that is to say, administered by Christ; not a material ordinance but a spiritual act, His act of joining us to Himself.

From our side, we enter in by our faith in His saving Name, by our reliance in response to that act of redeeming love; this is our part in tying the knot of union with the Lord.[1] Or again, otherwise, regarding the matter from the view-point of outward order, we enter in by our "baptism into the Name" of salvation. For that baptism "visibly signs and seals" (Art. xxvii.) all the promises to faith, and embodies them; and so it is to our possession of Christ as the patent is to the nobility, as the sealed deed is to the house and land.

So viewed (to pause yet a moment before our paraphrase proceeds) our blessed Baptism is "the outward and visible sign" of "the circumcision of Christ." That "circumcision" is a thing greater, deeper, more divine than any outward rite, Mosaic or Christian. It is the real "death to sin and new birth to righteousness" wrought in man by the almighty grace which makes him a living, believing member of the Christ of God. But baptism

---

[1] See Bishop Hopkins (of Derry, 1690), *On the Two Covenants.*

is its outward counterpart. It puts the holy Thing into symbol, and seal, and embodying visibility, at the command of the Lord Himself. So it is in a true sense *the successor* of the circumcision of Moses, while it is *the symbol* of the circumcision of Christ. Yet all the while, let us keep our thoughts clear on the inmost truth of the matter. The circumcision of Christ is nothing short, is nothing less, than that "passing from death unto life" which grace grants to "him that cometh unto" Jesus. "Verily, verily, I say unto you, He that heareth My word, and believeth on Him that sent Me, hath everlasting life, and shall not come into condemnation; but is passed from death unto life" (John v. 24). So we proceed.

Ver. 11. **In whom. too,** "in" this wonderful Head, ("in" Him, for the very crisis now in view was your entrance "into" Him,) **you were circumcised with a circumcision not done by hand,** not of the material order, no mere physical operation, **in your** (τῇ) **putting quite off**[1] **the body of the flesh,** finding a wonderful

---

[1] Ἐν τῇ ἀπεκδύσει τοῦ σώματος τῆς σαρκός. Ἀπέκδυσις is a strong word, a double compound; I have expressed this by "quite" in the paraphrase.—The evidence is against the

emancipation from the clinging power of temptation through the body, **in the circumcision of Christ.** "Of Christ"; for your "putting off the body of the flesh" was, from the divine side, an act, an operation, *done by your Lord* when you came to be joined in covenant to Him. It was a separation between you and the power and pollution of evil, wrought by Him in the act of embodying you as a believer into Himself. In that gracious act of love and power He took you into union with Himself as He died for you and rose again. You were made partaker of His atoning Death and of the Burial which sealed and as it were completed it; all its purchased pardon was now your own, and all the abolition of sin's claim upon the sinner; all the guilt, and all the enslaving power, were done away for you. And then too He joined you to Himself

---

reading, ἐν τῇ ἀπεκδ. τοῦ σ. τῶν ἁμαρτιῶν τῆς σαρκός: τῶν ἁμ. should be omitted, as probably a gloss.—The phrase thus presented is bold indeed; the regenerate man, in Christ, appears as *divested of the body*; which in St Paul appears to mean always the physical frame, though with a deep side-reference to its connexion with temptation and sin. Here it is "the body *of the flesh,*" *i.e.* as *conditioned by* "the flesh," which in St Paul commonly denotes the self-life; self-will, self-pleasing, as the outcome of our fallen state. Of the body thus conditioned the man is "divested," in the sense of his finding in Christ a strong deliverance from the assaults of evil through it.

in the fulness of His risen Life.  As He died for you, the law is at peace with you, and sin shall not reign in you; as He rose for you, you live because He lives, and with a life direct from Him. And of this spiritual miracle and glory your Baptism is God's own sign, and seal, and visible counterpart; such that we speak of *it* as if it were the regeneration-gift itself.  Thus then you were spiritually "circumcised," into the new Covenant of peace and

Ver. 12. life, when **buried along with Him in your** ($τῷ$) **Baptism**; a burial figured by your plunge in the baptismal pool[1]; **in which too**, in which baptismal rite, **you rose along with Him, by means of your** ($τῆς$) **faith in** (lit., "of") **the working of our** ($τοῦ$) **God, who raised Him from the dead**; "who raised Him from the dead and gave Him glory, that your faith and hope might be in God."

How strong is the emphasis laid here by St Paul, and not only here, on the holy Baptism of the Christian. Quite sure I am that by St Paul, and by the primeval Church generally,

---

[1] Beyond doubt the *ideal* of Baptism was immersion. There is no proof however that actual immersion was ever a vital necessity to the rite; the symbolical washing somehow would probably be enough for signification. The verb βαπτίζω is *certainly* not conclusive.

Baptism was not regarded as a quasi-miraculous operation, through which as an action, and necessarily at its very time, a spiritual revolution took place within the recipient, or a spiritual spark was cast into his life. My deep belief is that the true apostolic idea of Baptism was that of the "sealing ordinance." That view leaves absolutely free the sovereign Spirit's action upon the soul, and the soul's action Godward in the simplest coming to Christ for life. But then, it gives also and at the same time divine honour to Baptism. It makes it, to the full, God's own Sign-manual to His Word, God's own Seal at the foot of His charter of the salvation which is by faith. And thus it bids the Christian teacher and believer, in the full bright daylight of the Gospel of grace and faith, make much of Baptism, whether given to the adult as the sequel to faith or to the infant child of the Church in prospect of it. It bids him cherish the God-given Rite which, in the language of old theology, *salutem in rem ducit,* " *embodies* salvation," puts it as it were into the concrete, and says to the baptized, " As surely as your body received the water of the Covenant, so surely, so much as matter of fact, does your soul, through faith which rests on Christ, receive the mighty gift of the Covenant, its 'grace'—pardon, peace, new life, new creation, all things new."

St Paul now proceeds to tell the Colossians, in words of close personal application, more of what their Baptism means to them, thus viewed.

Ver. 13. **And you,**[1] you Colossians; let me speak without reserve of your awful original need of mercy; you, **dead that you were in respect of** ($\tau o \hat{\iota} s$) **your trespasses, and the uncircumcision of your flesh,** totally devoid of spiritual life, in any sense which could mean a power within you for revival and renewal; helpless and alienated, with an alienation evidenced by actual transgressions, and generally (is it not true?) by a life defiled by the dominion of "the flesh," the power of self upon the throne; you, thus circumstanced, cold and helpless in a

---

[1] The construction is carried on, and then dropt, and its direction altered. It is as if he would have written, $\tau o \hat{v}$ ἐγείραντος αὐτὸν ἐκ νεκρῶν, καὶ ὑμᾶς ἐν αὐτῷ. But he takes up καὶ ὑμᾶς as the point of departure of a new assertion: καὶ ὑμᾶς . . . συνεζωοποίησε.

spiritual grave, **He raised you together to life**[1] with **Him**, with Christ, (in the Resurrection of Christ, appropriated and as it were assimilated by you in faith,) **forgiving us**[2] **all those** (τά) **trespasses** of ours, those iron bars between us and our life and peace;

Ver. 14. **blotting out**, cancelling, **the bond**, the dreadful "note-of-hand" (χειρόγραφον), **couched in**[3] **the ordinances**, the statutes, precepts, of the eternal Law which we had broken, and which thus had a fatal claim upon us; the bond **which was directly** (ὑπ-) **against us**, inexorably demanding our satisfaction or our death; **and it**,[4] this condemning law, **He has**[5] **taken out of the midst**, out of the way, between us and a reconciled Father, **fastening it with nails to the cross** where the Lord died for us, the Just for the unjust, our Sin-bearer, stricken for our sins, that He might put their guilt away.

It is a wonderful picture. Behold the Cross of the Atonement, dyed with the blood of the Lord. Against it hangs, rent by the affixing

---

[1] Probably read here, συνεζωοποίησεν ὑμᾶς σὺν αὐτῷ.

[2] Read ἡμῖν. "He is eager to claim his share in the transgression, that he may claim it also in the forgiveness" (Lightfoot).

[3] So I attempt to express the "dative of relation," τοῖς δόγμασι.

[4] Αὐτό is slightly emphatic by position.

[5] The perfect ἦρκεν indicates an abiding result.

nails, a document. Approach and read; it is no less a thing than the Law of God! You wonder. Is it possible? Is it rightful? Is it not horrible? No; for that Law is there not in its character as the expression of the divine Will but as the covenant broken by the sinner, and therefore turned into his mortal foe, his sentence of second death. But the claim is met; the sentence exhausted. It has been done by our Head for us His members; by our "sacred Head once wounded" on that Cross. So now that "bond," *as to its hostility to our peace and salvation*, is dealt with and put aside. *As such* it is cancelled. The nails of the Crucifixion pierce it, to announce that it is cancelled, and to hold it up to view as the sinner's enemy no more.

Here is indeed "the wondrous Cross." What is it? No mere scaffold of the martyr, nor only the scene of a supreme example of love and fortitude stronger than death. It was indeed the instrument of an infinitely true Martyrdom and Example. But much more it was, for us, that quite different thing, the instrument of the propitiatory Sacrifice in which

"Christ redeemed us from the curse of the law, being made a curse for us" (Gal. iii. 13). And never shall we understand the true glory of the Example till we have seen something of the necessity and awfulness of the Propitiation, and have found in it, or rather in Him who "is the propitiation for our sins" (1 John ii. 2), our rest and life.

One further word the Apostle has to say here about that Cross. It was the implement of our most merciful deliverance. It was on its other side the implement of our Deliverer's mighty triumph over His enemies and ours, the powers of the dark Unseen. We infer from the words now to follow that they who, with their Prince, had so often crossed the path of the incarnate Lord, flocked as it were round His dying head in expectation of triumph over Him at last. They had long withstood the work of Redemption in its progress. They had ruined Paradise. They had drawn antediluvian man into monstrous sinfulness, till the race was all but blotted out.[1] They

---

[1] Is not the real reference to *them* in 1 Pet. iii. 19, 20? There is no proof that τὰ ἐν φυλακῇ πνεύματα means disembodied

had appeared in unprecedented force as possessing spirits just when the Lord walked the earth. Their Leader had tempted Him in the desert, and (may we not be sure?) had returned upon Him in Gethsemane. And now in the darkness round the Cross, so it would seem, the host of evil was present again. Will not the Son of Man at length be overwhelmed? Will not the Second Adam follow the First in his defeat, though by so different a path? No; the defeat is theirs, not His. He strips them, by His atoning death, of their spoils, their captives. He leads His conquered enemies along, disgraced for ever before the moral universe; and thus the Cross is the triumph-chariot of this wonderful Imperator.

Ver. 15. **Despoiling**[1] **the governments and the authorities**; the dreadful hierarchy of evil, bent upon

---

human spirits. They may well be the unseen adversaries of Redemption, to whom, in their dark world, the Lord in His intermediate State comes to proclaim (ἐκήρυξε) His victory over them.

[1] Ἀπεκδυσάμενος: the rendering, "stripping off from Himself," has been recommended; as a wrestler casts from him his disabled antagonist. The R.V. renders, "having put off from Himself," with the very improbable alternative in the

retaining us as their spoils, plundered from God; **He exposed them**, "made a shew of them,"[1] **with boldness**, with the open, outspoken (παρρησία) confidence of unquestioned victory, **holding triumph over them on it**; on, in, the Cross; His scaffold from one view-point, His imperial chariot from another.

Even so, Lord Jesus Christ. So didst Thou conquer; so were our deadly enemies trodden down under Thy sacred feet, yes, while those feet were pierced upon the Tree. Then let us appropriate and enjoy Thy victory, and bid meek defiance in Thy Name to the hosts of the darkness, within us and around us. "Jesus they know."

*Vicit Agnus noster; Eum sequamur.*

---

margin, "having put off (*His body*)." But the middle ἀπεκδύσασθαι could quite properly mean, "stripping them (of their possessions) *for Himself*." And this is surely much more in keeping with the context, where the imagery of a Roman triumph seems to be in view.

[1] The Latin versions have *traduxit*, the word which would be used of the procession of captives in a triumph at Rome.

He gave me back the bond;
It was a heavy debt;
And as He gave, He smil'd, and said,
"Thou wilt not Me forget."

He gave me back the bond;
The seal was torn away;
And as He gave, He smil'd, and said,
"Think thou of Me alway."

\* \* \* \*

It is a bond no more,
But it shall ever tell
All that I ow'd was fully paid
By my Emmanuel.

SABINE

MAKE me a captive, Lord,
  And then I shall be free;
Force me to render up my sword
  And I shall conqueror be:
I sink in life's alarms
  When by myself I stand;
Imprison me within Thine arms,
  And strong shall be my hand.

G. MATHESON, D.D.

# CHAPTER VIII

### HOLY LIBERTY IN UNION WITH CHRIST

##### COLOSSIANS ii. 16-23

ST PAUL has unfolded something of the treasures hidden for us in our Lord Jesus Christ. He has disclosed to us the bright depths of the divine "Fulness," all embodied in Him, so that we, being in Him, are filled full of It. He has told us that our union with Him is a spiritual circumcision, an act powerful for our purification, and also the pledge of all the gifts of the better Covenant. He has led us up to the Cross of Calvary, and shewn us there the death-warrant of the broken Law, pierced with the nails that pierced the Lord, cancelled for ever by His precious death in our stead; we, His members, enjoy the "forgiveness of all our trespasses" because our Head has suffered for them.  And then He has lifted the veil of the Unseen, to shew us the awful personal powers of evil spoiled of their prey, conquered in what seemed their hour of conquest, led along in triumph by our King, who has transfigured the Cross into the car of victory.

It is Jesus Christ, always and everywhere. The invaders of the Colossian mission had never indeed professed to banish Him out of their system; but they did not enthrone Him in it everywhere and always; and it is this which His servant cannot tolerate.  Such is Jesus Christ that He cannot but claim to be "all things in all things" to us, if we would be Christians indeed.  The programme of our personal religion must be nothing short of this, if we would find in it not merely a law for external performance but an inward joy and force.  Christ for us, Christ in us; this is religion at its heart, at its vitals.  Blessed are they who find this out for themselves under the illumination, under the anointing, of His Holy Spirit.

Before me on my table lies a paper of four pages, headed "Christ is all and in all."  It is just a collection of Scripture passages, arranged and combined, to set forth the Lord Jesus Christ as He meets the needs of the sinner. "Thou that believest on Him unto eternal life (1 Tim. i. 16)," so begins this paper, "meditate upon these things: Thy sins (Luke xv. 18)—Christ's cross (1 Pet. ii. 24): thy guilt (Rom. iii. 19)—Christ's righteousness (Phil. iii. 9): thy weakness (Rom. vii. 18)—Christ's strength (2 Cor. xii. 9): thy temptations (1 Pet. i. 6)—Christ's tenderness (Heb. iv. 15). . . . Remember this:—When thou hast sinned—Christ is thy Advocate (1 John ii. 1): when thou doubtest—Christ is the Truth (John xiv. 6): when thou changest —Christ is the Same (Heb. xiii. 8): when thou diest—Christ liveth (Job xix. 25): when thou art buried—Christ is the Resurrection (John xi. 25): when the world allureth—Christ overcame (John xvi. 33)." And so on, through one group and paragraph after another. "Think what thou hast with Christ"; "Think what thou hast in Christ"; "Think what thou art in Christ": such are some of the titles under which are grouped the words of hope, and strength, and great salvation. Then the texts of inference are given in turn: "Therefore—Abide in Christ (John xv. 4): Walk in Christ (Col. ii. 6): Speak in Christ (2 Cor. ii. 17): Work in Christ (Rom. xvi. 9): Occupy for Christ (Luke xix. 13): Rejoice in Christ (Phil. iii. 3): Suffer with Christ (1 Pet. iv. 1): Wait for Christ (1 Thess. i. 10): Watch for Christ (Matt. xxiv. 42)." So, with a group of promises about the longed-for Coming of the Lord, and a few lines of entreaty to "search the Scriptures diligently that thou mayest increase in the knowledge of Christ," ("feeding thy soul in the Word," "being filled with the Spirit," and remembering that "there is no knowledge but in the anointing,") the paper closes.[1]

This little document has lately, after a long mislaying, been in my use again, and it has been a "silent comforter" indeed, with the comfort which means strength for our exceeding weakness. It is an unpretending little thing

---

[1] I believe it is still to be had, on application to the Rev. J. E. Sampson, Barrow Cottage, York. But my copy is several years old.

in its form; very far from what is called scientific; just a collection of isolated Scripture texts, intended for the use of one who on the one hand knows himself to be a sinner, and on the other has had some sight of a Saviour, and who also believes simply that the Bible is the Word of God.

The very idea of the "isolated text" is now in some quarters deprecated, if not condemned; because of what is undoubtedly the fact—that the context of a text must not be forgotten. So this paper, "Christ is All," will certainly not command every Christian student's approval. Yet I dare to say that it has been to me like a clear voice from heaven, at a time of no small internal exercise and trial both of thought and feeling. Its "isolated" quotations, I cannot but remember, are in the very manner of our Lord and His Apostles.[1] And just because its sole purpose is to set forth the glory of Jesus Christ, it leads us with sure steps over the field of Scripture; for His own voice on the day of His Resurrection has told us that

---

[1] The New Testament is really full of illustrations of this.

in all the Scriptures are "things concerning Himself." To me, called as I am by duty to studies more or less accurate, and sometimes to the painful task of reading some work on religion which while as able as possible seems strangely devoid of Jesus Christ—this little paper has spoken with a sort of self-evidencing power, as it brings before me "Jesus only, with myself." It is a message to the very heart of life from the very heart of God; for it is altogether a presentation of the Name of His Son. It takes the soul up to a region far above "the strife of tongues," and "the pride of man," and the speciousness of keen but superficial reasoning—to a place where it is possible to "abide satisfied," "quiet from the fear of evil."

I mention this incident of private Christian experience just to emphasize the message which, if I read it aright, St Paul carries to us in this Epistle, and very particularly in these sections. He has to meet "the Colossian heresy." And he meets it all along, all round, and all through, with Jesus Christ, the All-satisfying, All-sufficient Saviour and Lord.

It is just HIMSELF; nothing else, nothing less. It is Christ, glorious and personal; not Christ as a mere formula for certain ideas, but the divine-human Lord, "in all things pre-eminent," in nature, in grace, in the Church, in the soul; for pardon through His Cross, for life through His Life, for glory through His Appearing. To have Him and make use of Him is peace, and power, and purity. To do without Him is impossible; it is death. To use Him only partially is perpetual unrest and disappointment. He must be "all things in all things"; then there shall be a great calm within, and a great strength and great holiness with it, and at last an "appearing with Him in glory," to crown the process, and give it its developement for ever.

Even so, Lord Jesus. Be nothing short of "all things in all things" to us, in this our Colossæ now, wherever it is.

The Apostle has something now to say to them about "Christian liberty," in connexion with his great theme. They were appealed to by the new propaganda to submit to a round of observances on Mosaic lines. They were taught that in order to be saved, certainly in order to be safe, they must keep the ancient precepts about ceremonially clean and unclean food, and about allowed and forbidden drinks. They must religiously observe the festivals of the Law—yearly, monthly, weekly. The Sabbath, for example, must be regarded in its strictly Jewish aspect; not as God's primeval gift to man, but as His token of covenant with Israel.[1] At every turn of life they must be careful, in this spirit, not to "handle, taste, touch," this thing or that thing, particularly in the way of food, which the Old Law (or in some cases the traditions that had gathered around it) had interdicted. And all this was with the hope that this series of denials, and abstinences, and "neglecting of the body," would promote its sanctification, and bar out the cravings of "the flesh." Moreover, they were told much of angelic powers, and of the duty of giving them devotion, and looking for their mediating aid as a path to God; a doctrine

---

[1] See further below, p. 175.

which would surely tend, like the asceticism of the same teachers, to keep the devotee away from a full and happy communion with his Redeemer Himself. All this St Paul meets with a strong appeal to the Colossians to hold fast their liberty, and not to allow themselves to be "judged" for declining to follow any guidance, whatever its authority might seem, the other way.

Only let us observe, before we approach the translation of his words, what was his real aim in them. They are indeed an appeal for " Christian liberty," as earnest, though less impassioned, as his appeal to the Galatians "not to be entangled again with the yoke of bondage." But let us note well that the " liberty" he means is the very opposite of licence, and has nothing in the world akin to the miserable individualism whose highest ambition is to do just what it likes. The whole aim of St Paul is for the fullest, deepest, and most watchful holiness. He wants his Colossian converts above all things to be holy; that is, to live a life yielded all through to their Redeemer, who is also their Master. He wants them *really* to deny "the indulgence of the flesh." He wants them to live not as their own but as the living limbs of Christ their Head—a life very far indeed from a self-pleasing and self-ordered one. His desire for them is not that they shall assert *themselves* against these alien emissaries, and trumpet forth their independence for their own sakes; "we were never in bondage to any man." He longs for them that they shall assert their LORD as their all, first to their own souls, then to any who would rob them of Him, and Him of them. He knows perfectly well that the prescriptions of the Judaists (his own experience is conclusive for this) will never make men really holy, for they will never make them happy and at rest in God. So he bids them resist this message and these claims, not for the sake of human rights, (momentous things in their place, but not in point here,) but for the sake of Christ's rights, and of that blessed bondage to Him which alone is perfect freedom.[1]

---

[1] *Cui servire est regnare:* the Latin original (cent. v.) of the phrase in the English daily Collect "for Peace."

Let us see well to it that such is our aim too in any resistance we may ever be called to oppose to any form of "spiritual despotism." Why, in the last resort, do we resist? Because of the dignity of manhood? That is a great thing, rightly understood. But the one fully true answer must be, Because of the rights of Jesus Christ over me, so that nothing must be allowed to cross and hinder my immediate contact with Him, for life, holiness, and service. Such a motive will make the assertion of "liberty" an act of allegiance, and will govern and chasten its whole character. From the point of view of the assertor, it will save him from the mischief of a really self-willed attitude. From the point of view of the testimony, it will save it from the weakness and coldness of a mere negative: it will elevate it into the assertion of a glorious positive—Christ is All.[1]

---

[1] It is too often assumed that the great word "Protestantism" carries "the weakness and coldness of a mere negative." It may be only too much so when it is misrepresented in word and spirit by some who bear the name Protestant. But historically it is a word full of the noblest positive elements. The great *Protestatio* of 1529, at Speyer,

Now we may resume our translation:

Ver. 16. **Do not therefore**, in view of such a position as we hold in our sacrificed and victorious Saviour, do not **let any one judge you**, take you to task, make you feel wrong and in disgrace if you do not obey him, **in eating, or in drinking**; forbidding you this or that sort of food on ceremonial grounds[1]; or **with regard to** (ἐν μέρει: "*in the class of*") **"Feast Day**, the yearly festivals of the Law, as Passover and Tabernacles, **or New Moon**, the monthly festival, when of old the trumpet was blown, and the offerings offered (Num. x. 10), **or Sabbath**, the weekly
Ver. 17. festival in its Jewish aspect[2]; which insti-

---

was a calm and truly Christian assertion of the *positive fact* that God bids all His people seek His will in His holy Word.

[1] It is almost needless to point out that such a practice as that of "total abstinence" from strong drinks, either for our own safety or for example to the tempted, is a matter remote from the connexion here. Very probably the new teachers at Colossæ did prohibit wine (as it was prohibited to the Nazirite in the Mosaic Law). But this would be on strictly ceremonial, not philanthropic, grounds. St Paul himself could say (and in an Epistle where he also strongly asserts "liberty," 1 Cor. x. 29) that if such or such a kind of food "*stumbled* his brother," really causing the man to violate his conscience, he would "*eat no flesh for ever* (εἰς τὸν αἰῶνα)" (1 Cor. viii. 13). The man who "totally abstains" for the sake of others takes that ground. And in the present state of our country I, for one, think that he rightly takes it.

[2] "The original, σάββατα, is a Greek plural in form, but

tutions are indeed[1] **a shadow of the coming things**, the things which were once in the future, the things of the Gospel, foretold by prophets and outlined by institutions—as a shadow is cast by a solid, and in a

---

only as it were by accident. It is a transliteration of the Aramaic *shabbâthâ* (Hebrew, *shabbâth*).

"It is plain from the argument that the Sabbath is here regarded not as it was primevally (Gen. ii. 3), 'made for man' (Mark ii. 27), God's benignant gift, fenced with precept and prohibition only for His creature's bodily and spiritual benefit; but as it was adopted to be a symbolic institution of the Mosaic covenant, and expressly adapted to the relation between God and Israel (Exod. xxxi. 12-17); an aspect of the Sabbath which governs much of the language of the Old Testament about it. *In that respect* the Sabbath was abrogated, just as the sacrifices were abrogated, and the New Israelite enters upon the *spiritual realities* foreshadowed by it, as by them. The Colossian Christian who declined the ceremonial observance of the Sabbath in this respect was right. An altogether different question arises when the Christian is asked to 'secularize' the weekly Rest which descends to us from the days of Paradise, and which is as vitally necessary as ever for man's physical and spiritual wellbeing" (Note in *The Cambridge Bible for Schools, etc.*).

We may add that it is, if possible, *more* necessary than ever, in these days of extraordinary high-pressure upon human life. "The Sunday superstition," as some are pleased to call it, is in reality the strong tradition of reverence for a precious gift of God, old as the race, and capable of ever-growing developements of benefit.

[1] Ἅ ἐστι: ἐστί is very slightly emphatic by position; I have represented this by "indeed." He means to acknowledge in passing the real place and value of the Festivals *as* "shadows."

measure indicates its shape—; **but the body is Christ's**; the Reality which projected the shadow is His, for it is in fact Himself, in His redeeming work and glory. "His atoning Sacrifice, His Gift of the Spirit, His Rest, are the realities to which the old institutions pointed." If you have HIM, you have *in that respect* got beyond *them*.

Ver. 18. **Let no one have his own way in robbing you of your prize,**[1] your crown of life and joy at the Coming of the Lord, in the way of **humility,** (the artificial humility of the trained devotee, a self-abasement before unlawful objects, not the true humility of a soul at the feet of Jesus,) **and worship of angels,** the unauthorized *cultus* of those who are

---

[1] Μηδεὶς ὑμᾶς καταβραβευέτω θέλων: we cannot discuss fully here the rendering of this difficult sentence. Only let us observe that (*a*) καταβραβευέτω means (by usage) simply to frustrate the competitor for a βραβεῖον or prize in a contest; it does not mean to decide (βραβεύς), as a judge or umpire, against the competitor: (*b*) the words ἐν ταπεινοφροσύνῃ κ.τ.λ., following θέλων, *may* be construed *with it*; the rendering then being, "Let no one rob you of your prize, *taking pleasure in humility*," etc. (see Lightfoot, who advocates this rendering). The construction is supported by the Septuagint. Yet it is without any New Testament parallel, and seems to us less likely than the easier rendering adopted in the text above. According to this, St Paul would charge his opponents not indeed with directly wishing to rob his converts of their salvation, but with a purposeful effort to controvert their belief of truths which as a fact were saving.

but the Lord's "ministering spirits" for His people's good[1]; **invading things,** regions, **which he has not seen,**[2] **getting inanely inflated** (φυσιούμενος, present participle) **by the mere mind of his flesh,** the unconsecrated exercise of thought in the unregenerate state; wandering afar in speculations and imaginations which have not God but man for origin, and which therefore cannot humble, chasten, hallow, the

---

[1] Angel-worship was largely developed in the later Judaism. —It is remarkable that the Asiatic Churches seem to have been early and widely affected by it in sub-apostolic times.— Quesnel, the saintly Jansenist (Roman Catholic), says here, "Angels will always win the day over Jesus Christ despised and crucified, if the choice of a mediator . . . is left to the vanity of the human mind."

[2] Here a very difficult question of both reading and rendering presents itself. The "received text" has ἃ μὴ ἑώρακεν ἐμβατεύων. But there is important evidence in favour of the reading ἃ ἑώρακεν ἐμβατεύων, which gives of course the just opposite meaning. In the first case the teacher ἐμβατεύει what *he has not seen;* dealing presumptuously with mysteries of the unseen and eternal as if he knew all about them. In the second case he ἐμβατεύει what he *has seen,* that is, probably, alleged visions and revelations; things which he asserts himself to have "seen," or which he may really have "seen," but under the influence of deluding spirit-powers, alien from the revelation of Christ. On the whole, while recognizing the difficulty of the critical question, I recommend the retention of μή and the first alternative rendering accordingly. (See Appendix L in *Colossians, Camb. Bible for Schools, etc.*).—The verb ἐμβατεύει may mean, by context,

thinker, but can only inflate him in his own esteem;

Ver. 19. **and not holding fast** (κρατῶν), in his faith and in his teaching, **the Head**; the blessed Lord who is (i. 18) "the Head of the body, the Church," in all things pre-eminent, vitally and for ever necessary to His followers for both life and light; **out of whom**[1] **the whole of the body,** (not one iota can be excepted,) **through its** (τῶν) **joints and ligatures,** through the coherence of each "member" with the vital Head,[2] **getting supplied and getting braced together, grows with the growth of God,** developes a holiness and power of which God is Source, and Secret, and Environment; "nothing between."

---

either *to inhabit* or *to invade.* Retaining μὴ ἑώρακεν, "*invading*" will be the natural rendering of ἐμβατεύων.—Some scholars (as Lightfoot) suspect a corruption of the text in this difficult sentence, and would read ἀέρα κενεμβατεύων, "treading an airy void"; or the like. But the reasons for suspicion do not seem to me conclusive.—See Lightfoot here, and Westcott and Hort, *N.T. in Greek*, ii. 127.

[1] Ἐξ οὗ: the masculine pronoun, though the related noun κεφαλή is feminine. A Person is in question. Cp. the masculine pronouns ἐκεῖνος, ὅς, with the neuter Πνεῦμα in John xiv.-xvi.

[2] Rather (*in this connexion*) than with each other. The whole stress of the imagery, which necessarily outruns the physical conditions of the human body, is upon our *immediate* connexion in divine life *with Christ.* Thus the ἀφή and the σύνδεσμος are each believer's contact with and bond to HIM.—See the close parallel passage Eph. iv. 16.

Is all this so? Is your union with the Lord so close and so pregnant? Have you in you a secret of life and developement which is nothing less than God? Have not your new teachers manifestly travelled, and sought to lead you, to a lower level, and to a remoter distance from that blessed Centre? Then be on the watch against all that they would teach as their distinctive message. They profess the power to show you a way to purity through an elaborated asceticism and its rules. But in Christ you have already leapt to the centre of which such ideas, at best, are but a far-away circumference. In His death you, joined to Him, died too. His atonement set you wholly free from sin's condemning claim. And the power of His presence as the Crucified while Living Lord within you is the supreme secret for your emancipation from sin's hold upon the will. Use HIM against "the flesh." "By His SPIRIT mortify the machinations of the body" (Rom. viii. 13). This will be "victory and law," when lower expedients will fly in the hour of temptation like dust before the wind. So he proceeds:

**Ver. 20.** If,[1] as is the case, (εἰ with indicative,) **you died with Christ**, in His atoning and sin-condemning death for you, **from the rudiments**, the elementary lessons, **of the world**, so as to have got beyond the preparatory institutions of an order comparatively unspiritual, **why, as if you were still living**, finding your true life (ζῶντες), **in the world**, in that now obsolete and superseded order, **do you give yourselves to ordinances** (δόγματα), seeking salvation in a round of imposed and directed practices, in a discipline of meat and drink supposed to sanctify the soul? Why do you seek spiritual life in the watchword,

**Ver. 21. Handle thou not, nor taste, nor** even **touch the thing which is** "**common and unclean**"?[2]

**Ver. 22.** (**Those things** (ἅ), the things affected by these purely ceremonial prohibitions, **are all intended for corruption**, the corruption of consumption, **in our** (τῇ) **use of them**; "all meats" (see Mark vii. 19, reading καθαρίζων) are now given by the Maker and Master for His servants' natural use.) Such prohibitive formulas are after all **according to**, on the scale and level of, **the injunctions and teachings of mere men.** Yes, even such of them as once had divine sanction have it now no more, since their

---

[1] Omit οὖν from the Greek text.
[2] Cp. our Lord's own words, Matt. xv. 1-20; and see Acts x. 14, 15.

transitory purpose has been fulfilled in Christ.[1]

Ver. 23. **Such-like things** (ἅτινα), principles and expedients like those now pressed upon you, **do indeed possess a pretension** (λόγον: "repute" without reality) **to wisdom, in** the cultivation of **will-worship,** a devoteeism invented and elaborated by human choice, **and humility,** of that plausible but spurious sort denoted just above (ver. 18), **and unsparing treatment of the body;** practices which look at first sight as if they *must* be cognate to a true victory over evil, but which all the while, as compared with our glorious Secret, are **not of any value against the indulgence of the flesh.**[2]

Here is the *envoi* of the intricate and pregnant paragraph. Below it all has run the urgent moral problem, How shall I meet and conquer the indulgence of the flesh? No mere abstract question is in view: this is no competition of theories in the air. The most

---

[1] And many of the ascetic rules were from the first man-made only. See the closely kindred passages, Matt. xv. 9, Mark vii. 7; with Isa. xxix. 13, to which they refer back.

[2] So the R.V. translates the difficult clause. This rendering, and this alone, seems to give full coherence to the passage. It was suggested long ago in Conybeare and Howson's *Life and Epistles of St Paul*. Bishop Lightfoot amply proves its grammatical lawfulness.

awful of realities was before St Paul and the Colossians; the presence of sin, the power of temptation, the mystery of our moral bondage in the Fall. To the question which it perpetually put at Colossæ, and which it puts to-day and here to my readers and to me, the new teachers in the Asiatic mission (and they have always had successors everywhere) sought to reply by a process. They advocated ceremonial precepts, disciplined devotions, severities upon the body. St Paul knew well what they meant, for he had in the past gone far beyond them on their own ground. And he was still as sure as ever that we are called, in Christ, to a life which must be always watchful and always self-controlled; the exact opposite of a self-seeking independence. But he had learnt, in the light of the Lord, that the heart of such a life is found in the holy liberty wherewith Christ has made us free, by making us one with Him. The man, kept awake by grace to his own awful weakness and to the foes that beset him, will indeed not only pray but watch. But he will do so as one whose secret and resource of moral power in the watching life is altogether Jesus Christ our Lord. He will oppose HIM to the enemy, who seems sometimes all but omnipotent. He will draw upon his HEAD for the strength and victory which shall make the weak " limb " able to " do great acts." He will retire into CHRIST, and abide there, for deliverance and peace, that he may continually serve Him in holy purity in the stress of real life. He will remember that in CHRIST he died, in CHRIST he lives. And his life now, yea, in this formidable " flesh," will be lived in peace and power on the ascetic principle of heaven—" by faith in the SON OF GOD, who loved me, and gave Himself for me."

Thou to us, O Christ, art given
  Force and freedom still to be;
Let us ante-date our heaven
  Evermore by trusting Thee;
    Thee opposing
  Always to our enemy.

# THE ROOT AND FRUIT OF HOLINESS

> Go up, reluctant heart,
> Take up thy rest above;
> Arise, earth-clinging thoughts;
> Ascend, my lingering love.
>
> BONAR.

Looking up for the Spirit through Jesus Christ is the only effectual attitude for obtaining love to God.

CHALMERS.

# CHAPTER IX

## THE ROOT AND FRUIT OF HOLINESS

### COLOSSIANS iii. 1-7

Ver. 1. **If therefore,** since therefore (εἰ with the indicative verb), **you did rise along with our** (τῷ) **Christ,** in that resurrection of which your baptismal emersion (ii. 12, 20) was the pledge and seal, a resurrection which meant at once your state of acceptance for His death's sake and your share in the power of His endless life, **be seeking now the things above,** the things on high, **where our** (ὁ) **Christ is, at the right hand of our** (τοῦ) **God seated;** enthroned with Him, as at once your Intercessor, Head, and

Ver. 2. King. **On the things above set your mind,** the bent and tendency (φρόνημα) of your thought and will, **not on the things upon the earth,** whether they be earthly gain or glory, or earthly expedients

Ver. 3. for moral strength and victory. **For you did die,** when the Lord died for you, and when you, coming to Him, identified yourselves with Him in His death. Then did you, in Him, die to sin's condemning claim, and so find the secret, in Him, of a "death" to sin's allurements and sin's tyrannies alike; looking down on them all as from the Cross to which sin nailed your Lord, and where He cast its load away from you for ever. And that death, because it was "with Christ," in union with Him, was followed of course by life, by resurrection, by part and lot in His own immortal and victorious state as the Risen One; you died, **and your life lies hidden**, stored, safe-guarded, once placed there, secure for ever, **with our** (τῷ) **Christ in our** (τῷ) **God.** There it lies, and there it lives; and so if you would *live it out*, using this wonderful life-power for spiritual triumph and service here on earth, you must go evermore to find it there; you must "seek" it; you must "with Him continually dwell," in steadfast recollection, simplest reliance, and ceaseless secret reception of the divine supply. And remember meanwhile that all this present process is working towards a mighty issue, which is meant to animate

Ver. 4.   to-day your every thought and effort: **when our** (ὁ) **Christ shall be manifested**, disclosed (φανερωθείς), at His glorious Return, in all the splendour of what He is, this Christ who is **our**[1] **Life, then you also with Him shall be manifested in glory.** All that He was in you shall burst from its bud into the fulness

---

[1] He has just said "*your* life"; now he "hastens to include himself among the recipients of the bounty" (Lightfoot).

of its eternal flower ; it shall be seen *what* such a Head has been doing all along for His members, as He gave Himself to them in their life of need and of faith. You shall be manifested with Him, He shall be manifested in you. Then see that you use Him as your life to-day, in the uplifting hope of such a to-morrow. "When He shall appear, we shall be like Him ; for we shall see Him as He is. And every man that hath this hope in Him purifieth himself, even as He is pure" (1 John iii. 2, 3).

This is one of the golden paragraphs of the whole Bible. To countless hearts it is one of their peculiar treasures. There is a celestial music for them in its very phrase and rhythm. It lifts the soul as with wings, till we get a glimpse of that exalted One sitting throned after death at the Right Hand of power, and in some sense realize that where He is we His people are, as to the true heart and basis of our regenerate being, and *know* that that basis is nothing less nor lower than HIMSELF, and stand upon that fact, and look out from it towards the coming glory, and turn to a renewed and joyful walk here, " in this present world," by faith in the Son of God.

It is a passage memorable for its messages to servants of God. Stevenson Arthur Blackwood, of ever bright and blessed memory, always referred to the words, "*Your life is hid with Christ in God*" as the means of his conversion. William Pennefather, in the church at Barnet, gave out these lines of Newton's Hymn, ("Rejoice, believer, in the Lord,")—

> "Your life is hid with Christ in God
> Beyond the reach of harm;"

and the Spirit brought them home to the asking heart in a final crisis of glad assurance. Who does not know that fear often lies near great joy, and that a treasure may seem far too precious to be safe? But here, he felt, was a safety equal to the treasure; "with Christ in God," a double rampart, all divine.

A beloved and honoured friend of my own, now doing a great work for God, (and may it be continued into distant years, if our Master tarry yet,) has told me how, early in his course, those five words, "*Christ, who is our life,*" were made a new world to him. As he walked back to his home over the dark fields from a mission-service he had been conducting, these simple, these familiar words passed through his soul in one of those moments of insight which God alone can explain. "Within ten paces, as I walked, life was transformed to me," he said; so wonderful was the discovery that the Lord Christ is not merely Rescuer, Friend, King, but Life itself, Life central, inexhaustible, "springing up within my heart, rising to eternity."

For us too, writer and reader, may the paragraph bring its moments of insight into the full glory of grace and the full assurance of the hope of glory.

Meantime let us not forget that the whole paragraph is written with a certain purpose. It comes to us in organic connexion with the close of the previous chapter; and we remember in what direction that passage ran. It was altogether upon the problem, how to be holy, how to deal with "the gratification of the flesh," and to live a life pure and victorious, worthy of the child of God. This is full in view here Accordingly we remember that all St Paul says here of mysteries and glories, all his presentation of our death and our resurrection with Christ, and of our eternal life hidden with Him, and our coming manifestation in the endless bliss, is matter as practical as possible. It all means an answer to the question, "How shall I deal with the gratification of the flesh?"

So viewed, the passage loses nothing of its exaltation and charm of thought. But it becomes as different as possible from a mere golden reverie, in which the man attempts to escape from realities into the evening clouds, or tries to take a sort of opiate against earth's trials and temptations, compounded of imaginations of heaven. The verses are a chain of God's indissoluble facts, for the Christian's use amidst the formidable facts of the devil, the world, and the flesh. It is in order to his walking at liberty, in holy purity, in holy love, that he is (not to imagine, but) to recollect that because Christ died, *he* died, and is in that sense dead; dead to sin's doom, and to sin's dominion, in his crucified Lord. It is for practical holiness, for the life of open eyes and conquering hands in the way of righteousness, that he is (not to imagine, or "feel," but) to recollect—for it is fact—that because Christ rose, *he* is risen, and has within him the very "power of the resurrection" of his Head. He is to "seek the things above" with the most practical intentions. He is to "seek" them —as the needle "seeks" the pole—with the "search" of earnest thought and expectant faith, not as things only whose hope may cheer his faint steps onward, but as things whose present power is to make his steps sure and strong. For what are those things above? The throne of all love and power; the Saviour seated on it, triumphant for His follower, and faithful to him; and the life hid there with Him in God; yea, He who is Himself the Life. Sure of his own death with Christ, and his new life with Christ, in a union with which heights and depths of distance have absolutely nothing to do, he is to be always, at the back of everything, *there*—where Christ, his Life, is seated; where his true life is "hid," hidden, yet so as to be always as truly in the limb on earth as in the Head in heaven. And as he looks forward to the "glory that shall be revealed in us," it is to be with the same object, sure and certain, even a present holiness. He is to use the power he has, in having the crucified and glorified Christ for his Life, all the more confidently and promptly because of its foretold developement—" with Him in glory."

Here is St Paul's programme, his prescription, for the blessed life, the transfigured life, at Colossæ. Live in heaven, that you may really live on earth. Live in heaven, not in the sense of the poet but in that of the believer. Live in recollecting and conscious union with Him who is there, but who is at the same time in you, your Life. Live in the continual confession to your own souls that you died in His death, and live in His life, and are with Him—by the law of union—on His throne; and then bring *this* to bear upon the temptations of your path. *Use* these things. Take them as facts into life, exactly as life is for you to-day. You shall find that in them, that is to say, in HIM, you can be holy. You can walk at perfect liberty, and you can walk (with the same steps) in perpetual and delightful service.

"Touch not, taste not, handle not. Do not forget the new moon; be careful over the ritual of circumcision, and its obligations; invoke religiously your guardian-angel; in brief, be the punctual devotee." Such was the prescription of the Judaistic teacher, "with a view to dealing with the gratification of the flesh." And many tried it. But in the depth of the heart they found it "not of any value." Perhaps it gave some of them the poor and dreary boon of a restless sort of self-satisfaction, always suspicious of itself, and the more suspicious in proportion to the man's depth and sincerity. It hardened many of them perhaps into the miserable attitude of a proud rigorism; they looked with contempt, avowed or not, upon souls and lives supposed to be weaker and more lax. But one thing assuredly it did not do, for it could not; it did not make the votary holy. It did not cleanse the "first springs of thought and will." It did not produce the fruit of Paradise, "love, joy, peace, longsuffering, gentleness, goodness, fidelity, meekness, temperance" (Gal. v. 22, 23), *at the centre of the soul*, so as to fill the circumference of the life. It did not make the Christian utterly distrust himself, yet habitually overcome his mighty enemies. It did not teach him how (Phil. iii. 3) to "worship God in the Spirit, and rejoice in Christ Jesus, and have no confidence in the flesh." It did not make him at once supernaturally sweet, and supernaturally strong. For the secret of this lies not among "the things on the earth," the methods of a man-devised asceticism and ceremonial. It lies deep among "the things above, where Christ is, sitting on the right hand of God."

Let our programme be that of St Paul, for his is that of the Holy Ghost. Our aim, our longing, our hunger and thirst, is for a holiness which shall indeed be real, real before God in its root, and real before man in its fruit. We seek a holiness which shall win the world to own that Christ can make a poor human life blessed and fruitful, loving, cheering, useful, humble, tender, while yet strangely strong, with a power not its own, to rebuke the evil which it meets. We want to be holy in a way which shall never glorify ourselves, but always our Master. We want to have "a heart" that does " not condemn us " (1 John iii. 21); not the delusion of a supposed sinlessness, but the happy, honest certainty that the central and steadfast desire *and choice* is to please Him, to do His dear will. Then let us *go up*, to fetch our secret down. *Sursum corda.* Believer, your talisman for that life, the only " life worth living," is in the heaven of heavens. It is seated on the right hand of God. It is— " Christ which is your Life." It is He, as He died for you, as He lives for you, as He lives in you, as you live in Him, as He is coming for you, as you are going to be glorified with Him. " Seek HIM," with the seeking which is also a perpetual finding ; and use HIM as He is so found ; and you shall have your desire.

And now, as if to keep us close to the thought of the practical, St Paul goes on, dealing in a way as explicit as possible with the sins from which Christ is able altogether to deliver us. Let us follow him, step by step ; carrying with us, all along, " the things which are above." So shall we read to blessed purpose, and not merely to assent, to regret, and to despond.

Ver. 5. **Give to death therefore your limbs which are upon the earth**; "your limbs," your body in its details, viewed as the peculiar avenue and seat of temptation through the passions; "upon the earth," as contrasted with that Secret for victory and liberty which, as we have just seen, is found among "the things above." And then by a rapid step of thought he describes the "limbs" in terms of their sinful *functions*, the transgressions which are peculiarly and distinctively corporeal in their conditions. **Fornication, impurity, passion, fierce sensual craving, evil desire**, (for "desire," ἐπιθυμία, may be pure and holy as well as "evil,") **and carnal greed**,[1] for it is (ἥτις

---

[1] Πλεονεξία: "Lightfoot here sees a reference to covetousness in its ordinary sense; 'the covetous man sets up another object of worship besides God.' And he shews clearly that the Greek word never, *of itself*, denotes sensual lust. But compare this passage with Eph. iv. 19, ['to work all uncleanness with greediness,' μετὰ πλεονεξίας,] v. 3, 5, ['fornication, and all uncleanness, or covetousness,' πλεονεξία,] 1 Cor. v. 11, ['a fornicator, or covetous,'] 1 Thess. iv. 5, 6, ['not in the lust of concupiscence . . . that no man . . . defraud, πλεονεκτεῖν, his brother in the (τῷ) matter' in hand,] and it will appear that the word at least lends itself to *a connexion* with sensual ideas" (Note here in *The Cambridge Bible for Schools, etc.*). —The "idolatry" in such a case is a sensuous admiration easily developed into still grosser thoughts and feelings.

Ver. 6. ἐστίν) **idolatry; on account of which things the wrath of God,** the personal moral indignation of the Holy One, no figure of speech, no mere formula for processes of unconscious cause and effect, **is coming,** is already on its way, heralded by His warnings, till in the great crisis it shall fall **upon the sons of disobedience,**[1] the human allies and followers of Rebellion against God's will of Holiness. And let the remembrance of your own past fill you not with the Pharisee's scorn of the "rebels" around you, but with wondering gratitude and godly fear;

Ver. 7. **for these transgressions are things in which you too walked,** acted, behaved, formed character, **once, when you had your life in these things** (ἐν τούτοις): ἐζῆτε, not merely "lived" in the sense of "existed," but "had your life" in the sense of interest, motive, congenial atmosphere. When such ideas were your native air, you shewed it in the complexion of your conduct.

Let us pause here for the present. In another chapter we will take up the closely connected passage following.

Observe this glorious paradox, the placing

---

[1] Some important documents omit these last words; Lightfoot thinks that they are probably an insertion from the closely parallel passage, Eph. v. 6. But R.V. retains them.

close together, and in the most living connexion, of the two paragraphs we have just now translated. The first has taken us to the throne, to the ascended Lord, to the hidden life, the life hidden indeed, stored and treasured with the Son in the Father. The second takes us at one step into "the world which lieth in the wicked one" (1 John v. 19). It places us in thought not merely in the presence of sin, but in the presence of *such sins*—the crudest, the most outrageous, the most defiant and overmastering forms of evil. Here are things so strong in their grasp upon our fallen race that alas even in the fullest light of Christendom legislation dares not go all lengths in punishing them as crime; the thief must suffer where the fornicator may practically go his way. And who shall estimate the dreadful power of these serpents and scorpions in that old and effete world at Phrygian Colossæ? There the soft climate of the Levant combined with generations of political death and social inertia to foster every growth of moral weeds; and there was no tradition of Christianity, however distant and defective, to hold sin in that sort of check which our Christian tradition does apply, feeble as it too often is. What was to happen to these converts, just emerged from the fetid swamps? Were they to be nursed by slow degrees into some approach to health? Should they be educated little by little into small improvements, till a public opinion should arise at last which would help the feeble individual? Not so. St Paul knows "a way more excellent." He leads them straight from the fever-jungle to the heaven of heavens for the secret of a new life. GOD has worked in them the miracle of the first step; they have believed, just as they are, in Jesus. And none less than GOD will now work in them the miracle of that wonderful second step, the use of their union with Christ so as to tread, in their utter weakness, but in His Name, "upon serpents, and scorpions, and all the power of the enemy." They are entrusted at once with the whole secret, the inmost secret, of the boundless power latent in our union with Christ by the Holy Ghost. They are called upon at once to use it, and to live now, henceforth, in a humble, holy, glorious deliverance from their "tyrant lusts."

That secret is old as the Apostles, and it is modern as this hour. I have heard of a mission-station on the Congo where a noble standard of Christian conduct is successfully maintained by the missionaries, among the converts so lately "walking and living" in the foulest air of tropical paganism. And their secret is the inculcation at once on the new Christian of the deepest principles of union with Jesus Christ. The man who has three times burst into anger is debarred from the Table of the Lord; "You need not sin so; you have the whole power of Christ with you and in you, not to do it."[1] And just the same facts of grace and triumph reach us from the great Victoria Lake. In the wonderful work done by our Lord through His servants in Uganda, especially during the last four years,[2] nothing is more conspicuous than this, "the

---

[1] I owe this fact to my departed friend Mr G. Wilmot Brooke, who laid his life down for Africa, on the Niger, at the age of less than thirty; 1891.

[2] This sentence was written in 1897.

demonstration of the Spirit." Our time has witnessed there the transfiguration of a host of recently heathen lives and characters into fine specimens of Christian holiness and stability; a scene worthy of the morning-time of the Church of Pentecost. And how? By the method of taking the converts as promptly and as explicitly as possible to "the things that are above" for their resource and strength in the midst of a world of sin. Union with Christ by the Holy Ghost, Christ dwelling in the heart, the believer dwelling in and with his glorified Lord, the Spirit in His fulness filling the life with the living Redeemer, this has been the missionary's secret for himself, and he has passed it on without reserve to his dusky converts, with results of untold blessing.

No method could be more apostolically orthodox. It is exactly the method of Colossæ.

Drawing to a conclusion, let us notice a point or two in detail in the paragraph last translated.

i. "*Give to death therefore*," νεκρώσατε οὖν. The phrase is strong, it is startling. Here is no precept of slow amelioration. Alike the verb and its form, νεκροῦν and its aorist tense, suggest ideas of deliverance as entire and as prompt and critical as can well be. Is the Colossian beset by sensual lusts to-day? Has he a dreadful inheritance of past vile habits upon him, and all the old temptations around him? But has he come to Christ, and been joined to Him? Then here and now, not only to-morrow and somewhere else, Christ is his Life. And having *that* Power within him, he can say here and now to the threatening but beaten tyrant, "I set my foot on thy neck, in my Lord's Name; I *give thee to death* this day." And Christ the Lord, one with that man in the union of the Eternal Spirit, can so deal with his will and soul that not only shall the enemy be repelled; he shall fall as one slain at the door where he tried to enter. He shall be "given to death."

Let us not make the mistake of forgetting other sides of truth. Whatever that " death " means, it means no such condition as that the foe may not instantly revive if the man walks on in any power but his Lord's for liberty and victory. Assuredly it does not mean that the man ceases to be *a sinner* in the sense of having no longer a ceaseless need of his Lord's propitiation, (for at least his "falling short of God's glory,") and of his Lord's presence to save him from himself. But this it does mean, that in Jesus Christ, One with the sinner who knows and trusts Him, there lies *quite ready* a power by which the oldest and the worst temptation may be laid at our feet as dead. In Him it is possible for the drunkard to walk past the horrid door of the house of ruin, loathing it instead of secretly craving once more to enter. In Him it is possible for the slave of vice, its helpless victim yesterday, to rejoice to-day with the whole choice of a transformed will in the blessedness of purity; condemning himself as he never did before, yet rejoicing in the undreamt-of entirety of his deliverance. The deliverance would be "too good to be true," if its secret were not among "the things above"; if Christ were not his very life.

ii. Lastly, side by side with these glorious calls to a walk so pure, strong, and happy in the Lord, let us not forget the faithful warnings of the Apostle. "*For which things' sake the wrath of God is coming upon the sons of disobedience.*" In our day, as a rule, little, very little, is said in Christian preaching about the moral wrath of God. One would sometimes think that we were supposed to have got beyond it; that fear, even such a profound variety of fear as the creature's shrinking before the indignation of infinite personal Holiness, had ceased to count among human motives. It is far otherwise as a fact. And it is certainly very far otherwise in Scripture. Let us be true to our one sure precedent, His Word. God forbid we should put His wrath where He never puts it—into antagonism with His redeeming love. But let us put it, humbly, tenderly, where He does put it—on its way to fall upon the sons of disobedience.

# MORE UPON HOLINESS, ITS RULES AND MOTIVES

Brethren, call'd by one vocation,
  Members of one family,
Heirs through Christ of one salvation,
  Let us live in harmony;
Nor by strife embitter life,
  Journeying to eternity.

Let it be our chief endeavour
  That we may the Lord obey;
Then shall envy cease for ever,
  And all hate be done away;
Free from strife shall be his life
  Who serves God both night and day.

            Massie, from the German of Spitta.

# CHAPTER X

MORE UPON HOLINESS, ITS RULES AND MOTIVES

COLOSSIANS iii. 8-17

"THE Christian character is an unsinning character." This is by no means to say that the man who is a Christian is an unsinning person. No, "if he says he has no sin, he deceives himself, and the truth is not in him" (1 John i. 8). But then, when he sins, he is out of character as a Christian. It is immensely important that he should remember this. Rightly remembered, it will both humble him and encourage him, with divine results.

I have no intention here of discussing a deep mystery. I wish only to point to great facts of the experience of the soul, and in this case to facts which, as so often, have to be taken each as true and vital, whether we can mentally reconcile them or not. It is a fact that if I assert myself to have no sin, I deceive myself. It is a fact that in Jesus Christ, as "a man in Christ," I am not only released from the guilt of sin—I am emancipated from its power. I am "well able to overcome"; I need not fall here, and stumble there, "in Him that loveth me."

> "How vast the benefits divine
> Which I in Christ possess!
> Sav'd from the guilt of sin I am,
> And call'd to holiness."

Nothing is more practical in the common round of life than the thought that in Christ we, unworthy sinners, have an unsinning character. If indeed we love HIM with a love worth calling love, that thought will be to us an inspiration; for it will raise our whole idea both of the rule and standard of conformity to His beloved will, and of our capacity in Him to follow after it. If I do not mistake, this one remembrance will do more than many glowing exhortations to keep us conscious of "the sinfulness of little sins," and of the blessedness of the life in which they really can be "laid aside." It will lift the all-important *average* of our daily and hourly aim, and of the loving hope of living nearer and nearer "up to it." It will call us with a voice divinely cheerful away from a dreary contentment with an inveterate experience of failure, and draw us close to the side of Him who can and will respond to our thirst for "a closer walk with God" in common things; making them *all* so many occasions for "walking and pleasing Him."

This view of Christian life animates the whole passage of the Epistle which we are now traversing. In our last chapter we saw St Paul applying the heavenly secret to the worst and foulest temptations. The "life hid with Christ in God" was there brought to bear upon "fornication, impurity, passion, and greed, which is idolatry"; all the grossest forms of confessed evil, things whose "inconsistency" with the Christian rule is flagrant. But St Paul has more to say now; he will come closer to the conscience, where it may be comfortably asleep. The Colossians must not be left for a moment uninformed that they are to carry, as Christians, an "unsinning character" into the every-day details of life, and are to live up to it in them all.  In Christ, as joined to Christ, as having Christ for their life, as looking to "the things above" for their secret of holiness below—they are not only to "do to death" such "members upon the earth" as fornication and pollution.  They are to "put off"—not merely to modify or reduce, but to put quite off from them—all sinning of the temper, all sinning of the tongue.  "The total abstinence of the Gospel" is to be the law here also; a law which *can be obeyed*, in Jesus Christ.

So he proceeds:

Ver. 8.  **But now**, as things are *now*, in your happy change of conditions since you ceased to "have your life" (ver. 7) in the old polluted region, **do you also**, you as all other true believers must do, **put away from you**[1] the whole list of sins (τὰ πάντα: "the all things," the many gathered up into a class), making no compromise, evasion, exception; counting nothing too common, too trifling, too passing, to be cast off *if it is not in the will of God*.  "Put away" (decisive word!) **anger, wrath,**

---

[1] Ἀπόθεσθε: observe the imperative. The English Version leaves it doubtful whether it is command or assertion: in the Greek, it is a most definite *command*, in the Lord's Name, to do a something which *can* be done, in His power.

alike the chronic (ὀργή) and the more sudden (θυμός) sort; **malice,** the ill-will, however concealed, which can wish the least evil to a neighbour; **railing,**[1] foul-mouthed talk (αἰσχρολογία ἐκ τοῦ στόματος ὑμῶν), at
Ver. 9. once abusive and defiling.[2] **Do not lie to one another, seeing you stripped off,** when you entered into Christ, **the old man with his practices,** the old state of the unregenerate; your state in Adam, not in Christ; the state of guilt under sentence and of bondage under temptation, with all the subtle "practices"[3] which it fosters in heart and life;
Ver. 10. **and did clothe yourselves with the new man,** (entering, in the second Adam, on your new state of acceptance and of spiritual victory,) that mystic "man" which **is being** ever **renewed,** ever maintained and developed, **unto spiritual knowledge,** so as to capacitate you for fresh intimacy with your God, **in the image of Him who created him;** so as to resemble more and more that FATHER who

---

[1] Βλασφημία: the Greek word means evil-speaking against either God *or man*. We have come to restrict "blasphemy" to the former. The context here makes it plain that the latter is meant.

[2] The word αἰσχρολογία in its general usage suggests both ideas together. I have attempted to convey this in the translation.

[3] See Rom. viii. 13 for the same word in a suggestive connexion: "If ye by the Spirit do to death the πράξεις of the body."

has constituted (ἔκτισε) you His children in His Son, and so has "created" that glorious phenomenon, Christ and His members, one Body.

Ver. 11. **There,**[1] in this happy region, in the life and society of the New Man, **there exists not**[2] **Greek and Jew, circumcision and uncircumcision, Barbarian, Scythian,**[3] **bondman, freeman;** such distinctions, *as things which can divide heart from heart*, cannot breathe, as it were, in the blessed atmosphere of

---

[1] I abandon here the Apostle's relative construction, ὅπου, for the sake of clearness in the extended paraphrase.

[2] Οὐκ ἔνι: more emphatic than οὐκ ἐστιν.

[3] "Greek," Ἕλλην, in such an antithesis as this, "denotes all nations not Jews that made the language, customs, and learning of the Greeks their own" (Grimm's *N. T. Lexicon*, ed. Thayer).—"Barbarian": "The word *barbaros*, in Greek, first denoted the speaker of an unintelligible language, and so a non-Greek, whatever his state of society or culture. It thus [at first] included the Romans, and in pre-Augustan Latin writers is even used as a synonym for Latin. [*E.g.* Plautus, in the prologue to one of his comedies, reminds the audience that the drama was originally Greek, but *Plautus vortit barbare*, "Plautus turned it *into Latin*."] But 'from the Augustan age the name belonged to all tribes which had no Greek *or* Roman accomplishments' (Liddell and Scott, *Greek Lexicon*)." (Note here in *Cambridge Bible for Schools, etc.*).—"Scythian": the "barbarian" *par excellence*. The Scythians were probably akin to the modern Turks.—There is evidence (from Herodotus, i. 105, 106) that in the time of Josiah the Scythians poured into Palestine, and made havoc of the country. Thus the name would carry a special sound of savagery to Jewish ears.

the New Man. National, and educational, and social variations of course remain still, as things in themselves; but as things which can interfere between member and member of Christ they are no more. Nay, rather, (ἀλλά), **all things, and in all persons**, in all persons joined thus together, are just—Christ. Such is HE to each one of His own that each is to all, the rest, only an instance of His life and presence; each sees HIM in all. "Facts of race, history, status, are not indeed contradicted, but they are overruled and transfigured into mere varying phases of a central union with the Lord, who shines equally through all His members."

To those who know anything of the main lines of ancient thought it will be unnecessary to dwell at length upon the moral and social miracle implied in such words as these. The Greek looked habitually on "barbarian" races as descended from an origin radically other than his own. And the Jew, though he knew better, from that divine Book which so jealously asserts the oneness of humanity, had allowed himself, as we know, to look on non-Jews as beings with whom it was a sin to eat. Into a world so divided against itself came the

Gospel of our Lord Jesus Christ, Son of God, Son of Man, Redeemer, Life, and King; and lo, within a few short years an ultra-Pharisee is writing thus to Grecized Phrygians. And the process has gone on, till every corner of the earth is now contributing its joyful illustration, and there is neither European, nor Asiatic, nor African, nor Indian of the West, nor Islander of the Oceans, but all, and in all, is Jesus Christ.

We must pass soon to another paragraph. But let us not leave this one without one more mindful look at its penetrating law of holiness, and at the motive and reason underlying. Shall we, my reader and myself, deliberately remember that *imperative* of the Apostle, ἀπόθεσθε, "*put off*," and the things which it includes? We have here before us, as we have seen, no longer sins of the scandalous order, as it is supposed specially to be. We are concerned only with the facile transgressions of the temper, and of the tongue; "anger, wrath, malice, railing," and talk that is not quite clean, and that is not quite true. Take this to heart, Christian man or woman, professing to "live godly" in common life in the modern world. The precepts given here lay hands upon a great many things tolerated all too easily at the dinner-tables, and in the drawing-rooms, and at the holiday resorts, of such as we are supposed to be. Our offences may not perhaps look great in point of scale. We may not be violently passionate, or positively abusive and indecorous in speech, nor may we be of those who deliberately "love and make a lie." But do we not too easily let ourselves sin on a moderate scale in things which are just the same in kind? We are irritable; we carry about a cherished grudge; we speak harsh words of the absent, when no good purpose whatever *really* underlies the speaking; we needlessly allude to uncleanness; we trifle with truth and manipulate it, when to do so will save us a little trouble. And all these things are identical in kind with the worst bursts of anger, or the most cruel objurgations, or the gravest falsehoods. They lie on the same inclined plane, away from the love of God, and towards the outer darkness. Then we will take no half measures with them. We will "put them away," just as we would put away a filthy garment, which it would be misery to wear for another quarter of an hour.

And what will be our motive and our power for doing so with such pollutions? Alas, in our own name and strength the effort will be vain. To the repressive exertions of self, the sins of self are like the shirt of Nessus upon the tortured and helpless Hercules. The very struggle, when conscience goads the unregenerate will, may even develope the *virus* of the habit. But the Apostle knows a better way. He gives the Colossians a command, but he supports it and makes it possible by a divine fact. He reminds them that *as a fact* they have passed from death unto life, and have exchanged condemnation and bondage in Adam for the pardon and the power which are in Christ. Whether they are subjectively "feeling it" or no, *this* is the objective fact and law of their position and of their condition; they are in Christ, and Christ is in them. And their brother-Christians are in Christ, and Christ is in every one of them. Let them recollect their own life in Him, and His in them, and they will bring in an invincible force against their sins. And let them recollect the life of their brethren in Him, and His in them, and they will need little else to teach them the lesson of unselfish love.

Nor let them think that the power of such a secret shall be felt only within the circle of the saints. Let it be *really felt there*, and it will be impossible to keep it from a gracious overflow upon all the world. To the Christian, every other man either is in Christ, or may be; he is a Christian *in posse*, if not yet *in esse*. For him, Christ died. In him, Christ yet may live, in grace, and in glory. Thus the Lord already looks upon His servant out of that man's eyes; that man has already Christian claims upon the Christian.

But now he passes into further details in the same line. And his tone is now positive. We have thought thus far mainly of "putting off." It is well, it is vital to do so. But it is not enough; it is to be done only in order to "putting on."

"I want that adorning divine
 Which only Thy grace can bestow;
 I want in those beautiful garments to shine
 Which distinguish Thy household below."

True, we have already had mentioned a noble "putting-on," that of the New Man. But this was a matter of position and of possession. There must also be the " putting-on " of realization, and of use, and of manifestation ; or the blessed means will miss its end.

Ver. 12. **Put on therefore,** clothing yourselves anew, **as God's chosen ones,** "chosen in Christ before the foundation of the world" on purpose to be like Him, **holy,** dedicated by that sovereign choice to Him, **and having His love set upon you,**[1] in that sublime original exercise of it; put on, I say, as your "beautiful garments," **a heart**[2] **of compassion** (οἰκτιρμοῦ, not οἰκτιρμῶν), sympathies ready and open, **sweetness** of temper and bearing, **humble-mindedness,** the attitude of a soul "which has lost its pride in discovering the mercy of its salvation,"

---

[1] I thus attempt to convey the force of the perfect passive participle ἠγαπημένοι. It is more than the verbal adjective ἀγαπητοί.

[2] Σπλαγχνά is better rendered so than as in A.V. The σπλαγχνά included *not* the bowels but the lungs and heart, the *viscera nobiliora*.

meekness in submission under pain and trial, **long-suffering,** the spirit which will not be tired out of pardoning, hoping, loving; **bearing with one another, and forgiving one another,**[1] if (the "if," ἐάν, puts, as it were reluctantly, a case just supposable) **any one has a grievance**[2] **against any one;** (for you are erring sinners still, and *may* give each other occasion for such victories of good over evil). **Just as the Lord,** (so read, probably, not "God,") the eternal Saviour *and Master*, with His infinite rights, **did forgive you,** as you rejoice to know He did, **so do you too;** using your assurance of pardon, your undoubting certainty that "your sins *are* forgiven you for His Name's sake," not for indolence and slumber, but for the glad activities of a self-forgetting kindness. **But over all these things,** as if it were the girdle upon and around all these graces, bracing them into one, put on **love,** which (ὅ, not ἥτις) **is the bond of perfectness;** for it makes and it maintains, as no other power can do, the "perfectness," the wholeness, the sweet ripeness of the Christian character, whether in the man or in the company. "Seeking its joy in the felicity of

Ver. 13.

Ver. 14.

---

[1] Ἑαυτοῖς: lit., "yourselves," but obviously (as in many other passages) in the sense of "one another" *in community.*

[2] The "quarrel" of the A.V. is Old English, from the French *querelle* and the Latin *querela*; not a wrangle, but a cause of complaint.

Ver. 15. others," it must be so, it will be so. **And let the peace of Christ ($X\rho\iota\sigma\tau o\hat{v}$, not $\Theta\epsilon o\hat{v}$) arbitrate in your hearts;** let every inward debate between self and God, between self and others, be ruled and guided by the deep consciousness that in Christ you are indeed at rest; let the plea for self-assertion be ever met and negatived by the decision of that umpire ($\beta\rho\alpha\beta\epsilon\acute{v}$ς) in favour of love. For that "peace of Christ" is given you not for yourselves only as individuals, but for the community; **into it you were in fact ($\kappa\alpha\acute{\iota}$) called,** at your conversion, **in one body;** you were brought one by one under its gentle power as those who were now one with one another in a society whose inmost law should thus be holy peace. **And be ye, become ye** ($\gamma\acute{\iota}\nu\epsilon\sigma\theta\epsilon$) more and more, **thankful;** prompt to see your mercies, and to praise the Giver—sure and blessed secret for a tone of loving and generous sympathy towards all.

Meanwhile, in order to the stability and depth of this life, where self was to be subject and Christ Sovereign, they were to fill their minds and souls with the articulate message of the Gospel. In order to enjoy "the peace of Christ" they were to be perpetually conversant with "the word of Christ." Their law of loving holiness, and their power to keep it, was to be no matter merely of impressions and sentiment. It was to be altogether conditioned by the revealed facts of their salvation; based always on that "word of God which liveth and abideth for ever," and which is so totally different a thing from the mere consciousness of even regenerate man; for it is the definite revelation given by the God and Father of our Lord. For the Colossians, that "word of Christ" would be largely given in the Old Testament Scriptures, full all through of "the things concerning Him." Then, it would be given also through the oral teaching of their inspired Missionaries, which for us exists now *only* in the form of the New Testament Scriptures. And already the New Testament Scriptures themselves were beginning to appear, and to be owned as "the word of Christ"; this present Epistle is an example, for assuredly it was read in the Colossian assembly with a reverence at least as great as that which the scrolls of Jeremiah claimed when they were first read in the Jewish Church. Doubtless we must not limit the phrase "the word of Christ" to written conveyances of the Lord's message; certainly not, while the Apostles and "apostolic men" were with the Church. But equally surely the phrase would suggest first and most in that day "the Scriptures of the prophets," as unfolding Christ,[1] and would then inevitably attach itself also to the indelible written utterances of the Apostles and Evangelists. For us yet more that "word" must mean the Scriptures, unless we are to drift we do not know where. Not as if "God were shut up within the covers of an old Book"; but as if He had, as He has, given us in that Book the one great articulate Letter He has written to His children, to be their perpetual certainty about His will, His heart, His way, His salvation, His Son. He is not "imprisoned" in His Letter. But none the less His Letter is absolutely unique as such. We have still, and always, to ask, in the last resort, "Is it written?"

Ver. 16. **The word of our ($\tau o\hat{v}$) Christ, let it dwell in you,** as a permanent part, always present, of

---

[1] See the closing words of the Epistle to the Romans.

your thought and affections; let it do this **richly**, abundantly poured into your memories, and coming out largely into your language; and let it be thus **in all wisdom**, "the wisdom that is from above," a thing infinitely higher than the finest tact of the critic, or the largest views of the philosopher. Seek and pray that you may not only know "the word" verbally, but may enter into it with spiritual insight, and use it with spiritual skill, for yourselves and others.

One particular outcome of such a rich indwelling will be the developement of the social, devotional, service of sacred song; the speaking out in this beautiful way of an inward treasure of truth which cannot be hid: **Teaching and admonishing one another** (ἑαυτούς: see note on the word above) **in psalms**, the songs of the Old Testament saints, **and hymns**, the inspired praises of the Christian Church, **and spiritual odes**, compositions developed by gifted individuals, on the theme of the great facts and truths of the Gospel[1]; **in your** (τῇ) **grace**, in the power of your Saviour's presence, **singing in your hearts**, (not only with your voices, though your voices *must* be used, if you are to help "one another,") **to our** (τῷ) **God.**[2] And **anything**

Ver. 17.

---

[1] The paraphrase is of course only a *conjectural* definition of the three kinds of song named here and in Eph. v. 19.

[2] So probably read; not τῷ Κυρίῳ.

whatever that you may do, in word or in deed, **let all things be in the Name of the Lord Jesus**; as it were, perpetually "quote Him as the Master who sets the task, and owns and uses the servant"; remembering as the deepest instinct of your lives that in everything and for everything you belong to Him; **giving thanks to our** (τῷ) **God, His Father** (omit καί before πατρί), **through Him.**

The long section allotted to this chapter of our Studies closes here. The precepts of general Christian holiness are almost done; we shall approach next the beautiful kindred passage where these principles are carried into the details of Christian home-life. Very little needs to be said by way of pointing the moral of the last verses we have read; only a few words on two leading points.

i. First we note with thankfulness this quite special injunction regarding the use of Christian psalmody. Nothing could be clearer than this Scriptural authority for hymn-singing and psalm-singing, as not merely a natural and pleasant thing, but a definite means of spiritual blessing. Full inspired sanction is given here on the one hand to the cultivation of God's gifts of poetic and musical form, in the entire conviction that they *are* His gifts, and meant by Him for a purpose. On the other hand the Apostle lays it solemnly upon us to see that these rich resources are used " in spirit and in truth." The great purpose of the holy melody, next to its being " unto the Lord," is to be the " instruction and admonition of one another." The psalm, the hymn, the song, if it is to be of the right kind, and rightly used, must be calculated for no mere ear-pleasing ends; it must be such as to convey eternal truth, strong, tender, uplifting, searching, directing; carried with felt delight into the inmost mind, as Christians hear Christians singing with them.

Alas for us when hymn or anthem is "rendered" with a lower aim. It may shake the minster-roof, but it will be silent not only before the Throne but in the conscience and the will. Well and blessed for us when, in the spirit of St Paul's welcome command, we meet for a service of genuinely holy song, whether in cathedral, or in parish church, or in the social circle, or in the family apart; and

> "Sing till we feel our hearts
> Ascending with our tongues;
> Sing till the love of sin departs,
> And grace inspires our songs."

ii. Lastly we observe, not for the first time in the Epistle, the emphasis thrown by St Paul upon the duty and the joy of thankfulness. " Be ye thankful"; " Giving thanks to God through Him." And we notice it as it stands here in deep connexion with the *community* of Christian life. St Paul is restless with the longing to *draw together* the hearts of the Colossian converts, and weld them into one. He has many things to say to this purpose. But he reiterates this, and closes with it; " Be ye thankful," " Render thanks." He is using here a truth which is as powerful to-day as ever. There is nothing more sure to isolate hearts than the spirit of complaint. There is nothing more sure to fuse them into a strong and happy oneness than the Christian spirit of thanksgiving.

# THE CHRISTIAN HOME

How sweet, how heavenly is the sight,
   When those who love the Lord
In one another's peace delight,
   And so fulfil His word.
SWAIN.

THERE'S no place like HOME.

# CHAPTER XI

### THE CHRISTIAN HOME

COLOSSIANS iii. 18—iv. 1

WE have followed the Apostle thus far in his lesson of Holiness, as it has to do with social Christian life in general. We come now to the application of principles to one all-important particular, holiness as lived out in the Christian Home.

It is remarkable that St Paul's Epistles to the Asian Churches, Ephesians and Colossians, are those in which alone we find a detailed treatment of this subject; unless we add to them the Epistle to Philemon, itself also a letter to an Asian convert; a letter dealing altogether with a domestic problem, and containing special greetings to members of a home. It has been suggested that in the social traditions of " Asia " a certain prominence appears to have attached to the family idea, and that this led the Apostle to speak with the more fulness of the holy motives and precepts which alone can clothe that idea in its realized beauty. It may be so. Or is it not possible that the incident of Onesimus' visit and his conversion may have guided St Paul's thought somewhat specially to the interior of home life at the moment when he was called to address the Asian Churches?

Whatever the occasion for these expositions of Holiness at Home, let us thank God for them, as for some of the chief treasures of His Word. For on the one hand the Christian Home is truly "the masterpiece of the applied Gospel"; the scene of the loveliest manifestations of its spirit, and then also the source, or reservoir, out of which its noblest influence is to flow around. On the other hand Home is the place of all others where it is most easy for us forgetful sinners *not* to live in the full light and power of the Gospel. It is the place where we most easily go off our guard; where small inconsistencies are most readily allowed to grow into habits; where the member of the circle may only too lightly act as if there were less need there than elsewhere of the fulness of the Spirit, the indwelling of the Lord in the heart, the surrender of the whole life to God.

It is a special gift accordingly, this gift of the Master's precepts for our life in Him at Home. It is not for nothing that the New Testament has more to say in detail on this theme than on other particular aspects of Christian life, the ordained Ministry of the Church alone excepted. We might have looked for minute directions as to the Christian's conduct in the walks of business, for example. We have as a fact scattered precepts everywhere bearing on that field of duty; but we have nothing connected and combined upon it. It is as if the Apostle was led to emphasize holiness at home as not only beautiful and right in itself, but the true nursery of habits of holiness everywhere.

As we approach the passage now before us, let us meanwhile recollect that it comes in close connexion with all that has gone before. The

Christian at home is taken for granted as already a Christian indeed. All the truths about the Lord's personal glory given us in chap. i. are supposed to be living in his convictions. All the treasures of grace in our covenant connexion with Him, unfolded in chap. ii. and onward, are supposed to be in his mind and soul. He is one who knows that in Christ, the Son of the Father, the Saviour and Head of the disciple, he died, he rose again, he lives, with the life hid with Him in God; and Christ is his life. He has made proof of these inestimable facts (not thoughts only but facts) upon the realities of temptation in general. Now let him find and manifest their beautiful power in holiness at home. So viewed, the passage is no mere aspiration. It is an ideal waiting for prompt and lasting realization; for the spiritual means to realize it are all provided, in the Lord.

Ver. 18. **Wives, be loyal to your ($\tau o\hat{i}\varsigma$) husbands,[1] as it is fitting in the Lord.** From one side, you and

---

[1] Ὑποτάσσεσθε τοῖς ἄνδρασιν. Omit ἰδίοις before ἄνδρασιν. I use the phrase "*be loyal*" as best, perhaps, representing

they are on the most absolute of equalities; for you are sacredly one. From another side, in God's order, while you are to them the most honourable and honoured of friends and counsellors, apart from all the blessed endearments of your union, yet they are the appointed and responsible *leaders*. "The husband is the head of the wife"; a headship sanctified to both parties by its revealed analogy to the headship of the Lord in relation to the Church.

Ver. 19. **Husbands, love your** (τάς) **wives**, with that pure, faithful, reverent love in which you forget yourselves in devotion to them, **and do not be bitter towards them.** Never for a moment let your leadership be mistaken for a right to irritability of temper and to the miserable spirit of domestic autocracy.

Ver. 20. **Children**, a word which by no means indicates only early youth, **obey your** (τοῖς) **parents in all respects** (κατὰ πάντα), with the manifest one limitation of supreme obedience to the eternal Parent in His law of holiness; **for this is well-pleasing in the Lord**[1]; well-pleasing to your heavenly Father's heart, as a manifestation of your true life "in" His

Ver. 21. Son. **Parents,**[2] **do not irritate your children,**

---

the idea of a "submission" which is absolutely different from service, and yet is the recognition of a God-appointed leadership.

[1] Read ἐν Κυρίῳ, not τῷ Κυρίῳ.
[2] Οἱ πατέρες: lit., "*fathers*." But the word πατέρες is not

do not *challenge their resistance*[1] by unwise and exacting interferences, so different from the steady firmness of thoughtful and responsible affection, **that they may not be out of heart**, discouraged under the chilling feeling that it is impossible to please, that the word of praise is never heard, that confidence is never reposed in their affection and fidelity.

Ver. 22. **Bondservants**, (and here he turns to the class embodied to him in Onesimus, and whose peculiar and difficult conditions give them a claim to fuller counsels,) **obey in all respects**[2] **your human lords** (τοῖς κατὰ σάρκα κυρίοις), your lords "according *to flesh*," for One only is your Lord in the sphere of *the Spirit*; **not with eye-bondage**,[3] the fidelity and diligence which depends only on inspection, **as menpleasers**, mere candidates for favours where no loving loyalty is felt to either the human master or the divine; **but in simplicity of heart**, with the genuine

---

seldom used, in classical Greek, of both parents; and so in Heb. xi. 23, where Moses is hidden by his πατέρες. In the light of, *e.g.*, the teaching of the Book of Proverbs on maternal authority, we are surely right in assuming that both father and mother are in view in a precept like this.

[1] The special idea suggested by ἐρεθίζειν.

[2] Observe the identity of phrase, to the son and to the slave. It does not degrade the son's "obedience"; it elevates the slave's.

[3] Ὀφθαλμοδουλεία: only here and Eph. vi. 6. Perhaps the word was coined by St Paul.

wish to do right, to be really serviceable, **fearing your (τόν) Lord**, with that "fear" which means no "torment," no shrinking, but a reverent devotion
Ver. 23. to His sacred will. **Whatever you do,**[1] all through the common round, **from the very soul work at it** (ἐργάζεσθε), **as to your (τῷ) Lord and not to men**; put your whole heart into it, as into His will,
Ver. 24. "good, perfect, and acceptable"; **knowing that from the Lord you will get**, get as your due (ἀπολήψεσθε), for He has made it your due by His gracious promise of it, **the exact recompense** (ἀνταπόδοσιν), faithfully measured out in remembrance of *every* item of loving obedience—the recompense **of the inheritance**, the inheritance of glory, the eternal Canaan of the saints. There the slave of man, so he has lived the life of the faithful disciple, shall be dealt with as *the heir* of God. His "recompense" shall be nothing less than the "inheritance" of the heavenly riches of his Father. **For Christ is the Lord whose bondservants you really**
Ver. 25. **are.**[2] **But he who does wrong**, who breaks

---

[1] Read ὃ ἐὰν ποιῆτε, omitting καὶ πᾶν.
[2] Τῷ Κυρίῳ Χριστῷ δουλεύετε: the words are freely paraphrased in my translation. But the point of them is best given thus; the strongest emphasis lies on the word Χριστῷ, and the meaning is that whoever is outwardly κύριος to the Christian slave, HE is the true Possessor, and will deal with His servant in His own righteous and infinitely generous way.

the heavenly Master's will by unfaithfulness to the earthly master, **will receive** a like punctual recompense of penalty for **the wrong he did,** from the heavenly Master, in just severity; **and there is no partiality** with Him. He will not condone the master's sin because he is a master. But neither will He condone that of the slave, sinning against his Christian light, because he is a slave.

And now let the other party hear the same truth;

Ver. 1. **Masters,** (and they are addressed *in the presence of their slaves,* as both classes meet in the Christian Assembly, and listen to the Épistle,) **provide** ($παρέχεσθε$) **justice and equity for your** ($τοῖς$) **bondservants**; see that they get it, as regularly as you "provide" food and clothes for them; utterly banishing caprice, arbitrary treatment, inconsiderateness, out of your conduct towards them; **knowing that you too have a Master, a Lord, in heaven.** Yes, remember *that* in all the relations of life, above all in those which tempt you to think yourselves sovereign; the result will be no anarchy, but a noble liberty and friendship, even where slavery as an external institution still survives. Let HIS sovereignty possess your inmost souls; it will only quicken your sense of responsible authority, but it will at the same time keep out of it effectually the poison of the despotic spirit.

We have traversed thus this apostolic picture of a Christian Home. It was written for Colossæ, but it was also written for all time, for us. To be sure, one prominent part of the conditions has changed totally for us; English Christendom has long repudiated the theory and the institution of domestic slavery; to our ears the very word "slave" is traditionally abhorrent. And this is the direct work of the Gospel, not of non-Christian civilization. The most advanced of the ancient civilizations, as we well know, not only never repudiated slavery but shewed no tendency to do so. The genius and culture of an Aristotle only lead him to philosophize upon the matter, and to discuss the inmost nature of slavery, in terms as ruthless as they are interesting. In order to abolish slavery, the irresponsible owning of one human being by another, it was needful that the Gospel should intervene, revealing to the world the fact that God had taken to Himself the human nature which was as much the slave's nature as the master's; that for slave as well as master Christ had died; that "all souls are His"; that in the

Lord Jesus the poorest and weakest becomes the very child and heir of God. Yes, it was impossible that slavery should *ultimately* survive alongside the religion of Christ Jesus; though it was no part of the work of that religion to proclaim a social revolution, which must have meant a universal Servile War, in order to realize its noble ideal.[1]

Yet it is obvious that the precepts which directly bear upon bondservice have a perfectly real application by analogy to the service of free contract. For while the servant (of whatever grade) is free to make or not make the contract to begin with, and free—as free as the master—to close it in a lawful way, and while his or her ultimate personal rights are never lost for a moment during the time of service, still the contract, while it lasts, *is* a bond. It is a bond on the master or mistress; but it is a bond also on the servant. The servant sells time, and thought, and power, whatever it may be, into the possession of another for that season; no doubt with large limits and

---

[1] On the whole subject, see further below, ch. xiii.

exceptions, yet with a real sale. And that fact carries just enough analogy with the old and now justly impossible *bond*service to give a real point in English life to every appeal of the Apostle in this passage. It gives his words a grave weight as they deal with the *duties* of service; the fidelity, the heartiness, the recognition of the master's rights and claims rather than those of self. It gives them a weight yet greater as they speak of that relation to the Lord Jesus as the true Master which can dignify, can glorify, the smallest details of even menial duty:

> "A servant with this clause
> Makes drudgery divine;
> Who sweeps a room as for Thy laws
> Makes that and th' action fine."[1]

Yes, the domestic servant of our free and Christian time may read these precepts with a sense of not the debasement but the exaltation of all true service.

And of course the message here given to the "masters" will come home with at least

---

[1] Herbert: *The Elixir*.

all its original force to the employer of service now, whatever the service be. On him, on her, fully as much as on the "master" of the old time, it is laid to " provide justice and equity " for the employed. And let them not forget that the literal rendering of the Apostle's words is "justice and *equality*." Yes, equality, not in the Jacobin sense of an artificial *égalité* which can never be realized until *men* have given way to manufactured automatons; but obviously in that of a noble consciousness on both sides that before GOD all men are equal, as bearers of that great thing, Human Nature, and that as Christians they are nothing less than "*one* in Christ Jesus." That fact is not meant to float in the clouds, nor even to be sung in holy hymns alone. It is to be lived into the common domestic day. And the result will be not a confusion of all social relations, equally uncomfortable on all sides, but a generous and friendly mutual respect, in the light of which social variations tend to lose all hardness, and can even enrich and elevate life.

But let us look again at this picture of a

Christian Home as a whole. Observe the perfect harmony of parts presented in it, and the secret of that harmony. Here, grouped together in a narrow space, constantly in contact, so constantly that friction is only too possible, are these many parties; husband and wife, parents and children, masters and servants; each pair of parties in closest relationship, but all also more or less touching the others. And it is the undertaking of the Gospel that this domestic world shall be a scene of pure love, and happiness, and right. What is the method for the realization? It is just this, that on each party is pressed home its own duties and the other's rights. The woman is frankly reminded of her husband's leadership, not of her own claims to a concurrent equality. The man is reminded of his wife's sacred right to his love, in all the Christian depth and grandeur and *dutifulness* of the word "love"; nothing is said *to him* about the assertion of his leadership. The son or daughter is commanded, without compromise, to obey; not a syllable is written about the rights of personality, however immature, nor about excuses for disobedience in the possible harshness of elders who cannot "understand the young." The parent is bidden with equal emphasis to avoid the miserable mistake of asserting within the home "the right divine to govern wrong"; St Paul is silent *to him* about the maintenance of that authority of which he has so urgently reminded the child. The servant is addressed at length upon his duty of entire, loyal, unselfish fidelity, and upon the certainty of *divine* penalties for failure; he hears nothing about the rights of man, nothing even about the essential wrongs of slavery. The master hears on his part not a word about his prerogatives; for him the one paramount thought is that he himself is, in no mere sentimental sense, a bondservant, and that his bounden duty is to see that his bondservants get all their rights fully at his hands; for inalienable rights they have; they are his equals in the balance of the Lord.

And is all this mere rhetoric? Is it Utopia, οὐτοπία, a scene that never was, and never will be? No; because of the Gospel which underlies the whole thing as its antecedent and condition. Schemes of perfect human concord, whether in the home or in the state, (and certainly in the Church,) which leave out the full Gospel, are predestined failures; they forget sin, and ignore its remedy; how can they but fail, while man is a sinner? But St Paul approaches the Christian Home through the fullest possible "truth as it is in Jesus"; and then it becomes not Utopia, οὐτοπία, the place that is not, but Eutopia, εὐτοπία, the happy place. A power is then introduced adequate to cause the happiness; for "Christ in you, the hope of glory," "Christ's peace, umpire in the heart," is a power which can really make men and women habitually forget their rights and remember their duties, on both sides, and all round. And *then* there is happiness indeed!

The beautiful ideal has been realized, from the first. Shall we listen to Aristides, the candid observer of the Christian life of the second century? An Athenian philosopher, writing about the year 130, he is probably the earliest of the "Apologists," or defenders of the faith and life of the Church before its heathen critics. And he speaks from the interesting standpoint of one who seems not yet to have identified himself formally with the believers. His picture of the brightness and beauty of Christian life, and let me add of Christian death, is the more remarkable; it is the voice of an observer more than of an advocate. Let us hear him as he describes some sides of Christian life [1]:—

"Now the Christians, O King, know and believe in God, the Maker of heaven and earth, from whom they have received those commandments which they have engraved upon their minds, which they keep, in the hope and expectation of the world to come; so that on this account they do not commit adultery nor fornication, they do not bear false witness, they do not deny a deposit, nor covet what is not theirs; they honour father and mother; their wives are pure as virgins, and their daughters modest; and their men abstain

---

[1] I use the excellent translation by Mrs Rendel Harris (*The Newly Recovered Apology of Aristides*, Hodder & Stoughton, 1891).

from all unlawful wedlock and from all impurity, in the hope of the recompense that is to come in another world. But as for their servants or handmaids, or their children, if any of them have any, they persuade them to become Christians, for the love that they have towards them; and when they have become so, they call them without distinction brethren. They walk in all humility and kindness, and falsehood is not found among them; and they love one another. They observe scrupulously the commandments of their Messiah; every morning and at all hours, on account of the goodnesses of God towards them, they praise and laud Him; and over their drink they render Him thanks. And if any righteous person of their number passes away from the world, they rejoice and give thanks to God; and they follow his body as if he were moving from one place to another. And when a child is born to any of them, they praise God; and if again it chance to die in its infancy, they praise God mightily, as for one who has passed through the world without sins."

One beautiful sentence, just later than this extract, I must transcribe for its own sake: "And because they acknowledge the goodnesses of God towards them, lo, on account of them there flows forth the beauty that is in the world."

It is something to read proof, in a passage like this, that in the sub-apostolic Church, amidst all its defects and struggles, lives so lovely were lived, and homes were to be found—apparently found very often—in which the ideal of the Apostle was so fully realized. Too often our "Church History" seems little but a rough and sombre tissue of heresies and persecutions. Happily, in spite of the inward and outward foe, the life hid with Christ in God was yet lived truly, openly, widely, in the old days.

But we need not go so far back for our illustrations of the Eutopia of the Christian home. Which of my readers has not known an example?

Nowhere, perhaps, has the beautiful ideal been so often and so well realized as in our own dear land in these latter times. We live in a period when Home is assailed from many sides. The popular novel holds up its sanctities too often to coarse unhallowed criticism. The rush of the age does what it can to undermine and invade its borders, and mingle it with the crowd. We sometimes talk as if "the charm supreme of home's unbroken ring" were a curiosity of the past, to be analysed and admired as a relic, as an old picture, but out of date as a living thing. It is not so. In uncounted instances, in quiet village, in clamorous city, the Christian Home survives, an immortal phenomenon. Numberless parents exercise at this moment all the authority of wise love over responsive and devoted sons and daughters, themselves setting in their home the fair example of an unvarying, tender, watchful fidelity of affection. In households far and wide the master, the mistress, and their domestic helpers, hold each other in attachment and honour, and realize a true identity of interests. But then, these homes resemble those of the first century, and the second, in the fact that Jesus Christ is recognized as their true Centre;

present and in power alike in parlour and kitchen; "unseen Listener to every conversation"; Master of each heart, and so of all the company; causing each to forget rights and remember duties; to live for others first.

Happy those who are permitted to form part of such a home, and, by the grace of God, to contribute to its being what it is. To them it is given not only to taste some of the purest happiness on this side the sky, but to form a reservoir of it for the lives of others all round. For such a home cannot by any possibility help diffusing blessings, temporal and eternal, far beyond itself. It is a deposit of the very salt of the earth.

But let none of us wait till in our case every one else in the circle is contributing to this result. To-day, just where you are, do you, Christian at Home, be doing your part fully and willingly; the less apparent cooperation there is around you, the more need for the gracious power to go out from you. And it *will* go out from you, husband, wife, child, servant, mistress, master, if Christ is in you, the hope of glory; if Christ is your life; if you, having died with your atoning Lord, have your life now hidden, with your glorified Lord, in God.

It seems to have been His custom, after spending the day at Jerusalem in works of mercy or duties of devotion, to retire in the evening to Bethany to lodge in the house of Martha. Blessed is that house where Jesus is received, and where He condescends to take up His abode ; where His presence is sought in daily prayer, where master and servants, parents and children, sit together at the feet of Jesus, and hear His word.

PROFESSOR SCHOLEFIELD.

*LAST WORDS ON PRAYER, CONDUCT,
SPEECH: PERSONAL MESSAGES:
FAREWELL*

THE union of Christians to Christ, their common Head, and, by means of the influence they derive from Him, one to another, may be illustrated by the loadstone. It not only attracts the particles of iron to itself by the magnetic virtue, but by this virtue it unites them one to another.

CECIL.

# CHAPTER XII

LAST WORDS ON PRAYER, CONDUCT, SPEECH :
PERSONAL MESSAGES : FAREWELL

Colossians iv. 2-18

Ver. 2. **At your prayer,** τῇ προσευχῇ, prayer in all the width and depth of its meaning, worship as well as petition, **persevere**; prayer is indeed a rest and joy, but it is also a duty, a work, a ministry, and so it calls for purpose and persistency ; **watching in it,** keeping wakeful "in" the strength of the holy exercise, against sin and for God, **in thanksgiving**; letting the spirit and action of gratitude as it were surround your watching and praying lives. Too often is thanksgiving forgotten, especially when the believer is under trial; let him recollect its preciousness and its power, and never pray without it. If there is nothing else for which he can give thanks, he has always God in Christ, and he has " that blessed hope," and he has the trial itself, which is sure to be somehow " precious " (1 Pet. i. 7). And

Ver. 3. do not forget intercession: **praying at the same time also for us,** your evangelists and pastors, who covet the aid of your petitions as a true power with God, **that our** (ὁ) **God may open to us a door for** (lit., "of") **the Word,** the message of His Gospel, **to speak the Secret of our** (τοῦ) **Christ**; the hidden "riches unsearchable," now disclosed, which are in fact Himself, His Person, Work, and Hope; **on account of which** Secret, because I have this and not a man-made doctrine for my message, and because the world does not love it, **I have been bound** with the chain which at this moment attaches me to my
Ver. 4. Roman keeper. Yes, pray for me, **that I may manifest it,** may make this Secret large and plain to faith, even **as my duty is to speak** it; for "necessity is laid upon me; yea, woe is unto me if I preach not the Gospel."

Meantime, as you pray, so live. Make it the whole purpose of your life to "shine for Christ."

Ver. 5. **In wisdom,** in the holy practical good-sense of sympathy, humility, fidelity, **walk,** carry on the intercourse of life, **with regard to** (πρός) those **who stand outside** the circle of faith; your pagan neighbours, who will so surely watch the life and temper of those who claim to have found man's true creed. Take pains over this; **buying out from** alien ownership **the opportunity.** Be ready to *pay for* occasions for witness for your Lord; pay watchfulness and recollection, and now particularly pay the price of careful thought how wisely as well as boldly to seize the hour for Him. Pay down the gold of a diligent study of the characters, the tastes, the interests, even the prejudices, of "those who stand outside," that you may the better win them by a witness which shall be perfectly courageous but manifestly considerate also. And when you talk with them, especially when you meet their questions, perhaps their cavils, about the Gospel,

Ver. 6. **let your discourse,** your account (λόγος) of "the hope that is in you," **be always in,** attended and hallowed by, the **grace** of God, the loving power of your Lord in you[1]; **seasoned with salt,** kept wholesome and also pleasant to the taste by the "grace" around it, which shall banish utterly out of it the impure motive and debasing allusion, and make what you say about the Truth attract the spiritual appetite of the hearer.[2] Such a rule of

---

[1] Bp Lightfoot explains χάρις here by "acceptance, pleasingness"; a well-ascertained use of the word. But such a meaning would have no parallel elsewhere *in St Paul*.

[2] A reference has been seen here, very naturally, to the "salt" of humour and pleasantry, which no doubt can find a lawful while guarded place in both public and private "talk" about the Gospel. But this use of the word is not so common in Greek as in Latin. And the Lord's solemn reference to the duty of His disciples to "have salt in themselves" and to be "the salt of the earth" gives a graver

17

speech will lead to the right way of dealing with non-Christian neighbours; **to know how you ought to answer each individual** "who asks you a reason of your hope" (1 Pet. iii. 15); having intelligent regard to his character and his point of sight.

The primary reference of this passage, where the tone of conversation is in view, seems (as I have indicated) to be to "apologetic" conversation, the "discourse" of the Christian when he is accosted by pagan enquirers or objectors. The Apostle's thought is of the right sort of "*answer*"; and he is anxious that the converts should secure this by a watchful use of the "occasions" for witness which are sure to arise, and above all by using them in the full and conscious possession of "grace" and with the wholesome "salt" of candour and conciliation. He assumes that every convert would covet *to be* thus an "apologist"; an expounder and vindicator of the truth, of the Lord, whom he had found. His life would mark him out for enquiry, so

---

turn to the word in apostolic language. (See Matt. v. 13; Mark ix. 49, 50.)

different would he be from his old self. And then he must be ready to avow why and how he was different. He had found access into the peace and into the love of a God supreme, eternal, holy. He had discovered Him in a Lord and Saviour who was at once celestial and human. He positively knew forgiveness in Christ, and equally well knew moral purity and liberty in Him, and had received the beginnings of heavenly bliss in Him; Christ was "in him, the hope of glory." And this Christ was ascertainable, historic. He was fact of earth as well as truth of heaven. Will not the enquirer also make proof of Him, make adventure upon Him, even as his neighbour in the same street of Colossæ had done, and had found it so good to do?

These "answers" would be something very different from mere clever repartees. But they would be totally different also from mere rhapsodies and harangues. They would have the pith and telling point of personality, personal witness to a Person and His work.

No Church History can tabulate the extent to which the vast spread of primeval Christianity was due to this local and neighbourly evangelism, in which man told man, and woman woman, in the same little country-town, what Christ was, and was to them. Assuredly the work done was vast and deep. Only, it was vitally necessary that in order to the full power of the witness the witnesses should, behind all their "answers," "continue in prayer and watch in the same."

In countless mission-stations of Africa, Asia, and America that work is still going on. But not there only. In regions nominally most Christian there are still the Church *and* the World; just as it was of old in regions most Jewish, most Mosaic. There is still the call to the Christian who really has found "the Secret of the Lord" to live a true witness-life, and to "know how to answer every man." Still must the disciple seek to live so that others, strangers to his bright, sacred talisman, shall care to know what it is, and shall ask what it is, sooner or later.[1]

---

[1] As I write (1898), a friend tells me of one known to him, totally sceptical while not unwilling to listen to Christian witness, but just now stumbled by the *listless air of a*

Still must he "continue in prayer, and watch in the same with thanksgiving," and "buy out the opportunity," and "walk in wisdom as regards those who stand outside" the happy circle of conscious faith and peace. Still must he see that his "word," when they give him the chance of speaking it, is the word of grace, and of salt. Let us arise, and shine, and awake to the duties and joys of witness.

But the Apostle hastens now to a close:

Ver. 7. **My position generally** (τὰ κατ' ἐμὲ πάντα) **shall be reported to you by Tychicus,**[1] **that** (ὁ) **beloved brother and faithful worker**[2] **and fellow-bondservant in the Lord;** true comrade of that other Asian saint, Epa-
Ver. 8. phras, similarly described above (i. 7). **Him**

---

*Christian congregation in Church.* "Can these 'Christians' possess any secret better than my reason gives me?"

[1] I put the verb into the passive, to preserve the order of the words.—"Tychicus is named also Acts xx. 4; 2 Tim. iv. 12; Tit. iii. 12. He appears to have belonged to the province of Asia and probably to Ephesus. He was evidently loved and honoured by the Apostle; was beside him . . . in his first imprisonment; and was faithful to the end. His name, though not common, occurs on inscriptions and on coins belonging to Asia Minor" (Note in *Camb. Bible for Schools, etc.*).

[2] Διάκονος by usage denotes *subordination* as well as activity. But we can scarcely convey this in one English word.

I am sending[1] to you for the express purpose that you may know (read $\gnwte$) our (read $\hmwn$) circumstances, and that he may encourage your hearts, with the strengthening $\paraklesis$ of Christian fellowship and personal witness. And he does not go alone;

Ver. 9. I send him with Onesimus, that ($\tw$) faithful and beloved brother, who belongs to you, a Colossian like yourselves; who "departed from you for a season that you may receive him for ever"[2]; all the things going on here they will report to you.

And what eager questioning there would be, in the Asian town, in the assembly gathered in Philemon's great room! How much there would be to ask, about Paul's health and comparative comfort, about the prospect of

---

[1] "Ἔπεμψα: "*I sent.*" But the epistolary idiom speaks from the point of view of the *recipient* of the letter. The Colossians when Tychicus came would say, "The Apostle *sent* you"; so the Apostle writes, "I *sent* him." Our idiom is otherwise.

[2] We observe that to the Church at large St Paul says nothing about Onesimus' delinquency and recovery, and his legal position. That is reserved for the private letter to Philemon. What he does say to the Church is not only a warm testimony to what grace had made Onesimus, but an indication of what the fellowship of those early converts was, knowing "neither bond nor free." It shews too how fully he reckoned on Philemon's Christian action.—See further, chapters xiii. and xiv.

his acquittal, about the hope of his coming yet at length to Colossæ, above all about the work of the Lord at Rome! But the salutations have to be duly conveyed now:

Ver. 10. **There greets you Aristarchus, my fellow-captive,** my fellow-prisoner in the Gospel *war* (συναιχμάλωτος, not merely συνδέσμιος),[1] **and Marcus the cousin** (ἀνεψιός) **of Barnabas**[2]; about whom

---

[1] Aristarchus is probably the man named Acts xix. 29, xx. 4, xxvii. 2. If so, he was of Thessalonica. He was seized by the rioters at Ephesus; an incident to which *perhaps* the word συναιχμάλωτος refers. Later, he returned with St Paul from Greece to Asia, and ultimately sailed with him from Syria to Rome.

[2] Named also (we may assume the identity throughout) Acts xii. 12, 25 (cp. xiii. 5, 13), xv. 37, 39; 2 Tim. iv. 11; Philem. 24; 1 Pet. v. 13. St Peter calls him "my son," probably in a spiritual sense. In the Acts, he accompanied and then left Paul and Barnabas when they visited Cyprus and Asia Minor; seven years later, after the separation of the Apostles, he attended Barnabas to Cyprus. Now, nine or ten years later again, he is the trusted helper of St Paul, and later again is with Peter at Babylon. Perhaps still later, in St Paul's last imprisonment, he is wanted by the great Apostle as "useful for personal service."—Tradition, beginning as early as the second century, makes him the writer of the Second Gospel, in some connexion with Peter (Eusebius, *Hist. Eccl.*, iii. 39). Later tradition makes him founder of the Alexandrian Church.

you received orders, on a previous occasion; if he should come to you, as he may do, for he is probably to visit Asia, give him welcome; he is again, after days of difficulty long past, in my full confidence and affection. Ver. 11. And Jesus too, Joshua, who is known as (ὁ λεγόμενος) Justus,[1] greets you. They, Aristarchus, Marcus, Justus, belong to the Circumcision; of Jewish faith originally, not pagans. And of that large circle of converts, here at Rome, they stand alone in their fidelity to me and the Truth; the "Circumcision" generally have taken the attitude of opposition[2]; these men alone are co-workers with me in the promotion of (εἰς) the kingdom of God, His reign in Christ over man; proving to me, as they have done (οἵτινες ἐγενήθησαν), a comfort, a solace to my heart wounded by many alienations and oppositions in that very quarter.

Ver. 12. There greets you further Epaphras, who belongs to you,[3] bondservant of Christ Jesus. And

---

[1] We know nothing more of this disciple. His first name, it is well known, is the Grecized form of Jehoshua, "Jehovah's Help." His second (Latin) name was in common use among Jews and proselytes, to denote the "Righteous" follower of the Law.

[2] Cp. Phil. i. 15, 16.—My paraphrase is of course a *conjectural* exposition. But something of the sort seems necessary to explain the strong assertion, οὗτοι μόνοι.

[3] See above, on i. 7.

his bondservice shews itself now in his toil of soul for you; **always wrestling on your behalf in his** (ταῖς) **prayers,** resolved, like the patriarch of old, not to "let the Lord go except He bless" you; **that you may stand fast, perfect, whole-hearted, impartially loyal, and fully assured,** sure of your ground and of your path, of your Master and of His call, **in every will of God,** in every part of His will, every detail, leaving nothing neglected and undone which is for you His will. **For I bear him witness that he takes great pains** (read πόνον), in this labour on his knees, **on behalf of you and of the** friends **at Laodicea and of those at Hierapolis;** the other mission-stations of your river-valley.

Ver. 13.

May our Master grant more followers of Epaphras to His Church. We live in a period which sees, amidst much to deplore, an infinity of loving and elaborate "painstaking" in the work of the Gospel, whether in our home Christendom or far away. The air of Christian life resounds, it is sometimes almost agitated, by the abundance of operations, organized or not, for every imaginable purpose of good. But it is to be much feared that the "wrestling" and the "painstaking" *of Epaphras* are not abundant in proportion;

and we cannot possibly do without them. Let us pray that we may pray. Let us give our hearts no rest till we know what it is to do what Epaphras did for the converts of the Lycus valley. He bore their souls upon his soul. He yearned with the deepest longing that they might be holy in the sense of a single-hearted and thorough loyalty to the Lord. And he carried this yearning continually and urgently to God in Christ, resolved to reach Colossian lives by way of the Throne. Shall not each of us begin, or begin anew, the same "painstaking," for home and household, for parish, for church, for school, for college, for mission, for the Christian world?

Yet again the greetings of the saints are to be given:

Ver. 14. **There greets you Lucas, Lucanus,**[1] **the phy-**

---

[1] "It is interesting to find the Second and Third Evangelists in one small group around St Paul here. Cp. Philem. 24; 2 Tim. iv. 11.—Lucas had accompanied St Paul to Rome; so the '*we*,' '*us*,' etc., of Acts xxvii., xxviii., implies. . . . He appears again in 2 Tim. iv. 11 as the one personal attendant of the Apostle in his last imprisonment. Tradition, vaguely supported at the best, says that he was born at Antioch in Syria; that he was one of the Seventy; that he was the

sician so dear to me (ὁ ἰατρὸς ὁ ἀγαπητός),[1] loved and loveable, tender and true; and Demas.[2]

There are some further salutations, to be passed on from Colossæ:

Ver. 15. **Greet the brethren at Laodicea,** (only twelve miles away,) **and Nymphas,** Nymphodorus, the leading Christian there,[3] **and the Church at their** (read αὐτῶν)

---

anonymous disciple of the Walk to Emmaus; or, on the contrary, that he was a convert of St Paul's. . . . Lightfoot points out that he appears here as *not* 'of the circumcision,' and therefore as a Gentile; and that this is 'fatal' to the tradition that he was one of the Seventy" (Note in *Camb. Bible for Schools, etc.*).

[1] "'Indications of medical knowledge have been traced both in the Third Gospel and in the Acts' (Dr F. W. Farrar). . . . 'St Luke's first appearance in company with St Paul (Acts xvi. 10) nearly synchronizes with an attack of the Apostle's constitutional malady (Gal. iv. 13, 14), so that he may [then] have joined him partly in a professional capacity. . . . St Paul's motive in specifying him as the physician may have been to emphasize his own obligations to his medical knowledge. The tradition that St Luke was a painter is quite late (Lightfoot)" (Note in *Camb. Bible, etc.*).—Dr Farrar remarks that to St Luke alone we are indebted for all we know *ab extra* about St Paul.

[2] It is impossible not to notice the reserved brevity of this mention. Was Demas already showing signs of the spirit which came out later, 2 Tim. iv. 10?

[3] We may fairly assume that he was the *Philemon* of Laodicea.

house, the congregation meeting where he and his family dwell, the gathered converts of that district of the large city.[1] **And when this (ἡ) Letter shall have been read where you are,** in your meeting at Colossæ, **take care (ποιήσατε) that it be read in the Laodiceans' Church**-assembly also, (for it touches upon needs and perils which are rife with them as well as you;) **and take care that the Letter from Laodicea,** the Letter which will be forwarded on to you from thence, **you also read;** it will supplement this more personal message to yourselves, developing its teaching about the Lord, and adding other matter with it.

Ver. 16.

It is more than likely that this "Epistle from Laodicea" is none other than our familiar "Epistle to the Ephesians." That Epistle, as it is well known, has been thought to be rather a Circular to the Asian Churches than a missive to the Ephesians in particular. It

---

[1] For similar "Churches in a house" cp. Rom. xvi. 5; 1 Cor. xvi. 19; Philem. 2.—Possibly the house of Nymphas was the *one* meeting-place at Laodicea; if so, the converts of the city are here greeted first individually, then as in assembly. But Laodicea was so considerable a place that the house mentioned may have been only the chief place for worship.

is devoid of personal and local allusions, though Ephesus was the scene of St Paul's longest pastorate; it treats altogether of grand general aspects of truth; and in the first verse of the Epistle the words "at Ephesus" are absent from some important ancient documents. To my own mind no theory of that Epistle is so reasonable as that which regards it as "sent to Ephesus in trust for all the missions of the Province." If so, it would naturally find its way ere long to the great centre of the Lycus region, Laodicea, and only from thence would be forwarded to the minor and more remote Colossæ. Once so forwarded, it would have the strongest possible claim to be read at Colossæ in close connexion with the more local Letter. Where the two coincide, as they do so interestingly in many places, there would always be some instructive *nuance* of difference in the expression. And on the supreme topic of the Work of the Holy Spirit, Colossæ would have everything to hear from "the Epistle from Laodicea."

One solemn personal message remained to be delivered. It concerned an individual, called by name; very probably the son of the honoured Philemon and of Apphia his wife (see Philem. 2); a newly ordained minister, it would seem, in the Church of Colossæ, or, as some have thought,[1] of Laodicea. Perhaps the Apostle had misgivings about the young pastor's entire devotion. Or he may have desired only to impress on him the sacredness of his charge as soon as possible after his entrance on it. For Archippus may have been ordained to fill the vacant place of Epaphras, lately withdrawn to Rome, and the yearnings of Epaphras over his beloved flock may have prompted the words. However, they stand here written; a message for all time to all who dare to undertake the pastorate of souls; a warning, solemn as eternity, not to do anything with their commission short of its " fulfilment."

Ver. 17. **And say to Archippus, See to the ministry**[2]

---

[1] But this is not probable. The message would scarcely have been given to him *through Colossæ* when he was at work some miles away.

[2] Διακονία: the word does not necessarily mean an ordained pastoral ministry. But the context is all in favour of such

which you received, παρέλαβες, received in transmission, **in the Lord**, in union with Him for His work, **that you fill it full**. Take it as it were a vessel into which is to be poured all your life, all your powers. Act up to it all round. In private conduct, in public diligence and fidelity, in witnessing, teaching, everything, let the circle of your "works" be "found perfect before God" (see Rev. iii. 2).

" A minister of Christ," says that pregnant Christian thinker, Richard Cecil, " is often in highest honour with men for the performance of one half of his work, while God is regarding him with displeasure for the neglect of the other half."

" Enter not into judgment with Thy servant, O Lord." "Take heed to thy ministry, O Archippus, to fill it full."

Then at last the Apostle takes the pen from the hand of his amanuensis, to add the

---

a reference; the διακονία is evidently one highly sacred and distinctive.—There is no necessary reference to the "diaconate" specially. The word is a largely inclusive one. Archippus appears to have been *the* pastor of the flock in question.

accustomed autograph (cp. Rom. xvi. 22; 2 Thess. iii. 17) at the close, the token of affection and the guarantee of authenticity. As he does so, the long chain which fastens him to the warder makes itself felt and heard; and with this comes up to his soul all that it means, the afflictions of the Gospel, the glory of being the suffering witness to his Lord; and the Colossians shall remember it too, and help him in it with their prayers.

Ver. 18. **The greeting, by my hand, Paul's. Recollect my chains. Grace be with you.**

Perhaps in large and laborious characters (he refers to his "large letters," to the Galatians, πηλικοῖς γράμμασι, Gal. vi. 11) the lines were traced, by the dim-sighted writer. But large or small, they were the greeting of a mighty human heart, filled with the Spirit of God, His chosen Vessel; a heart through which the Inspirer had now poured this precious Oracle of truth and holiness, the Letter to Colossæ, which is now "the Letter from ₍Colossæ," God's own Circular to our hearts.

Here we leave the Epistle to the Colossians. In imagination we watch the scroll carefully dried, and rolled, and tied, and sealed, and put into the loving care of Tychicus, and in due time carried by him over sea and land to the valley of the Lycus, to those readers now so long departed. "The grass withereth, the flower fadeth"; but not in the fields of the Word of God. There the pasturage is green every month, and the celestial flowers, growing from roots "fast by the fount of life," are all amaranths. Our "Studies" have dealt with a subject-matter "which liveth and abideth for ever," for it is nothing short of Jesus Christ. In the Epistle before us we have been all along "considering Him." HE has been the answer to every question, whether of truth or of life. We have gazed upon the majesty of His Person, on the mysterious glory of His Headship alike over Nature and over the Church, on His redeeming blood, on His life-giving life, on His enthroned rest above, on His promised return. We have seen in Him the inmost "Secret of God," disclosed for us. We have had a glimpse of the pure eternal gold of "the treasures of wisdom and knowledge" heaped and stored in Him, yes, of "all the fulness of the Godhead, dwelling body-wise in Him." We have seen Him as the mighty Basis of the Christian's standing; He has blotted out the handwriting that was against us, nailing it to His Cross; He has embodied us into Himself. He is at once the Power and the Law of the Christian life; He is the Peace of the Christian heart; He is the Lamp and Hearth of the Christian home. It is He who binds souls together, or rather as it were fuses them into one, till people as distant as possible in race and associations, like Paul and Onesimus, know and love each other as more than brothers. He is all things, and in all.

As then, so now. He is "the Lord of Time," being the Son Eternal. So we and the Colossians are neighbours and contemporaries—in Him. To our questions too He is the answer; the peace of our consciences, the power and purity of our spirits, the light and life of our homes, the star and sun of our everlasting hope. The old page lives to us, and understands us, and converses with us, "in the heart of Jesus Christ."

Whatever be our Colossæ, it is a place of peace and gladness. For we, like our brethren gone before, are in Colossæ indeed, but also, wonderful fact, "in JESUS CHRIST."

He help'd His saints in ancient days
  Who trusted in His Name;
And we can witness to His praise,
  His love is still the same.

His presence sweetens all our cares,
  And makes our burdens light;
A word from Him dispels our fears,
  And gilds the gloom of night.

                              NEWTON.

## THE EPISTLE TO PHILEMON:
## INTRODUCTORY

GRACE makes the slave a freeman. 'Tis a change
That turns to ridicule the turgid speech
And stately tones of moralists, who boast,
As if, like him of fabulous renown,
They had indeed ability to smooth
The shag of savage nature, and were each
An Orpheus, and omnipotent in song :
But transformation of apostate man
From fool to wise, from earthly to divine,
Is work for Him that made him. He alone,
And He by means in philosophic eyes
Trivial and worthy of disdain, achieves
The wonder; humanizing what is brute
In the lost kind, extracting from the lips
Of asps their venom, overpowering strength
By weakness, and hostility by love.

COWPER.

# CHAPTER XIII

### THE EPISTLE TO PHILEMON: INTRODUCTORY

ALONG with the Letter to the Colossians as a body there went what we should now call a Note to one of them as an individual. Philemon, a convert of some wealth and social standing, as we gather from the allusions to his extended beneficence, was the person addressed. The matter of the communication was in itself purely domestic; it was, the return to him, after intercourse with St Paul at Rome, of a fugitive slave, Onesimus.

In all probability Onesimus would be himself the bearer of the note, as his own passport to his master's indulgence—to his more than indulgence, to his welcome and to his love in Christ, if the Lord should speed the message.

From some obvious points of view, we may even wonder that such a private note should have taken its place among the holy Scriptures, presenting itself now for citation as an oracle of God. That it did so find place in the Canon, very early indeed, is certain; evidence is ample that it was there long before the close of the second century, when even the free-thinker Marcion admitted it into his "expurgated" list of Epistles. Origen, early in the third century, quotes ver. 9 and ver. 14 as Scripture. It is possible that in the Epistles of Ignatius, quite early in the second century, traces of its influence on phraseology are to be seen.

This is the more remarkable because the surprise I have referred to, the wonder that such a writing should rank as a Scripture, was widely felt in ancient Christendom. About the beginning of the fourth century (was it a sign of deterioration in the Christian instincts of that day, when the old simplicity of the Church had suffered much from its external prosperity?) we find such feelings alluded to by Chrysostom the preacher, and Jerome the student. Jerome says that "some will have it that it is not Paul's; others, that it has nothing in it for our edification"; and some thought that it was written by the Apostle at a moment when he was "not the organ of Christ's voice in him." Chrysostom, with characteristic fervour, denounces those who think the Epistle unworthy of Scriptural rank, "as concerned about so small a matter, and on behalf of an individual only."

A curious hint of such a feeling is given, if I am right, in the "title" of one of the Greek manuscripts of the Epistle.[1] As we have it, that title runs,

Παῦλος ἐπιστέλλει τάδε βέβαια Φιλήμονι πιστῷ:

that is to say, "Paul writes these sure words as a letter to faithful Philemon." But is this the original form of the title? The Greek strongly suggests the rhythm of a *hexameter verse*; it begins and it ends metrically, only breaking down in the word βέβαια, which

---

[1] Preserved at Lambeth. The copy dates from cent. xii. only, but may of course transmit a "title" originating long before that time.

refuses to scan. But suppose we drop the first syllable of that word, and read,

Παῦλος ἐπιστέλλει τάδε βαιὰ Φιλήμονι πιστῷ:

we then have a perfect line. And what is its meaning? To render it in its own metre—

"Paul on *a trifling theme* thus writes to the faithful Philemon."

The change, when it once occurred to me, (it may have occurred to others before,) seemed self-evidently right. And thus there appeared, strange to say, in the very manuscript, a depreciation of the Epistle; the scribe's mind, like the minds so severely censured by St Chrysostom, could see only *a triviality* in the case of a runaway Phrygian slave! Then came some wiser and more Christian copyist on his track, and with two strokes of the pen changed "trifling" into "sure," βαιά into βέβαια—but to the ruin of the metre!

Such an undercurrent of disfavour as Jerome, and Chrysostom, and this title, indicate, makes the place of the Epistle in the Canon only the more remarkable and the more secure. It was not for nothing that the little document, offering to many minds in the old world such a mark for criticism, was included by the Church in the Pauline catalogue, and never even for a time displaced. It would be interesting in the extreme to know by what process it first found its way there; but who can tell us now? We can only suppose that in the first place the private note was made public to the Church by Philemon; this indeed *must* have been the case; and it would be a noble evidence of the sympathy of spirit with which Philemon received his Teacher's letter. Then, surely, in that community so full of the life and love of Christ, the sacred truth as well as exquisite beauty of the letter was at once recognized, and its bearing upon the whole range of the charities of Christian life. It approved itself, probably without the least demur, as not merely a personal but an apostolic message to Colossæ; and so in time the Churches of Asia would come to know it, and so the Church universal.

Thanks be to God for the fact of its presence, now and for ever, in "the Scriptures of Truth." As I have said, it is easy to imagine the surprise which, we have seen, was felt about it here and there. But who that has penetrated one step into the spirit of the Gospel does not feel that such surprise is at best a shallow and surface feeling, and gives way at once to a sense as deep as possible of the fitness and divine significance of the Epistle as Scripture? Is there not a manifest providence in it as such? Put aside for the moment its high literary beauty, which alone may make us rejoice over its reverent preservation. Had it been expressed as uncouthly as it has been in fact expressed with consummate tact and charm, still it would have been eloquent of the will of God, of the mind of Christ. Nothing could more perfectly have illustrated the faculty of the heavenly Gospel to adjust its principles to the minutest details of human relative duty; to shew it in action as at the same moment constraining the conscience and opening the heart; whispering to every person in a domestic circle, "Do right, here and now, in everything," and in that very whisper making them all feel a oneness of interest and affection inconceivable except in Christ. Above all, how could the deep antagonism of the Gospel to the *spirit* of ancient slavery have been shewn so powerfully, so prevailingly, and at the same time with such tenderness and peaceableness, as thus?

Here are two parties face to face with each other; one is an injured master, the other a slave, a fugitive, and probably also once a thief. In law (and all the social traditions of the time gave the exercise of that law full scope) the slave was now in the grasp of the master—to be treated with a despotic power of punishment much greater than what we now allow a man against his horse or his dog. Philemon might practically do what he liked with Onesimus; not only inflicting on him the harshest common punishments, but putting him to torture, sentencing him to death, and killing him by inches.[1] This

---

[1] "I should think that *no treatment* of a slave by his master could come under the cognizance of a Roman governor. . . . Modifications of the old barbarity have been overrated. I doubt whether any prohibition of the arbitrary killing of a slave was *regularly* made before the time of Hadrian [half a century after St Paul's death]. Philemon

position of things between them rested on the basis of a vast and immemorial social institution. Practically, the voice of the whole human race affirmed then, and had affirmed from all time, the naturalness of slavery in some form; and the Roman world, "*the* world," affirmed it in the extremest and direst forms of the institution. Who does not know terrible stories of deeds done to slaves in that order of things, deeds before which the agonies of *Uncle Tom's Cabin* pale into moderation? For assuredly Legree himself would not have perpetrated cruelties which Roman gentlemen and noblemen inflicted without a qualm. Vedius Pollio, an associate of Augustus, kept a shoal of huge conger-eels in a tank in his garden; to these creatures he threw his offending slaves, to be killed and eaten. One day the Emperor was dining with him, and a slave in waiting dropped and broke a crystal cup; he was promptly

---

would have power, most likely, to treat Onesimus *exactly as he pleased*. (Dr E. C. Clark, Regius Prof. of Laws in the Univ. of Cambridge; quoted in the *Camb. Bible for Schools*, etc.; *Colossians*, p. 191.)

sentenced to the tank. The poor fellow's cry to the Emperor—not to be spared, but to be killed in some other way, did indeed move the Master of the world to bid Vedius set him free, and to abolish his menagerie of eels. But the imperial friendship was not withdrawn; Vedius was not out of society. Half a century later, just when St Paul was reaching Rome, four hundred slaves, men and women, including no doubt literary slaves of high culture along with the most menial, were executed in one scene of blood, under the express and deliberate sanction of the Senate, while the troops lined the streets to prevent a popular rescue. And why? Because their master, Pedanius, had been murdered by one of his household; under terrible provocation, if all tales were true. And "old custom," says the dispassionate historian,[1] required in such a case that the whole existing slave household should suffer death, as a deterrent.

Crucifixion, at the master's absolute sentence,

---

[1] Tacitus, *Annales*, xiv. 42.

was the common punishment for even petty larcenies by slaves. And it need not be said that other and more everyday penalties were cruel in proportion.[1]

Meanwhile the law and usage of slavery had the support of philosophic theory, which maintained an aboriginal and essentially natural place for slavery in the order of human life. Plato, in his ideal Commonwealth, gives slavery ample room, and the master who kills his slave, though regarded as a wrongdoer, is visited with only a *ceremonial* purification. Aristotle, in the opening pages of his " Polity," discusses the relation of slave to master as one of the foundations of society. He defines the slave as a being who is by *nature* the property of another; who is and has nothing outside that fact; who is merely, as it were, his master's limb, an extension of his master's physical organism, with the one function of capacity to do his master's pleasure. In

---

[1] For vivid illustrations see many passages in Dean Farrar's powerful story, *Darkness and Dawn*. In the course of the story, the Dean gives an imaginary account of Onesimus' career.

short, he is a human being devoid of all personal rights.

The uncompromising sentences are impressive reading from one high point of view. To the Christian who has entered at all into the mystery of the "service which is perfect freedom," *servire illud quod et regnare est*, the sacred bondage of his Lord, the Greek thinker's words have a striking and even thrilling applicability to the relation of the redeemed to the Redeemer. But from the view-point of man and man they are formidable words indeed; exactly fit to supply a supposed intellectual justification for usages of pitiless cruelty in the field of real life.

It is important to point out by the way how totally absent from the teaching of the Old Testament is the Aristotelian view of slavery. True, a certain type of slavery is freely recognized in the Mosaic legislation, and is explicitly dealt with. The fact must teach us caution as regards hasty denunciation of every form of compulsory service, as if *per se* it must under all possible circumstances be an outrage on humanity. But we observe that the main drift of the Biblical legislation is always towards the protection not of slavery, but of the slave. Not for a moment is the slave of the Hebrew owner regarded as other than a man, with rights; equal in his humanity to his master, and fully capable with his master of part and lot in the covenant-mercies of God. At the passover-feast a place with the family is accorded, without reserve, *not to the hireling who has made free contract*, but to the slave, born or bought. The tendency may be said to be far less to emphasize the helplessness than the privileges of the slave; he is the all-but-member not of the household only but of the family circle.[1] From some aspects his condition and position

---

[1] See *Does the Bible sanction American slavery?* an essay by Prof. Goldwin Smith (1863). It is a powerful and suggestive discussion of this and kindred matters. The author, by the way, points out with emphasis (the more remarkable as coming from the then leader of philosophical radicalism) the absolute refusal of our Lord and the Apostles to adopt or promote "the spirit of political revolution," though surrounded by every temptation to do so. They thus saved the religious movement from becoming a political one, and so from challenging a conflict with political force *on its own ground*.

are capable of far nobler uses and issues than that of the "employé" where *the sole* connexion between worker and workmaster is that of so much money given for so much time and labour.[1]

Our Lord and His Apostles take up and carry on the Old Testament ideal so far as to recognize and tolerate slavery as a fact in the world. But inevitably He goes forward, leading His disciples with Him, laying down with a new and divine emphasis truths which silently but surely were to discredit altogether the very idea of the purchase and possession of man by man. Not by revolutionary denunciation does He supersede the root-principles of slavery, but by the facts of His own holy Incarnation, meritorious Cross and Passion, glorious Resurrection and Ascension, and the coming of the Holy Ghost. Henceforth human life is to be seen and studied in the light of the glory of the Son of Man. So irradiated, our nature appears invested with

---

[1] See Dr C. H. Waller's *Handbook to St Paul's Epistles*, pp. 178, etc.

a majesty and a mystery which could not possibly be adequately perceived before; and man learns to look upon his fellow, whoever he may be, with a reverence which has done more for human liberties than all the rhetoric ever expended upon abstract rights or concrete wrongs.

This brings us back to the point we reached some way above, the beautiful phenomenon of contrast between this Epistle to the slave-owner Philemon, and the then current notions and usages of slavery. Here is the Apostle, engaged in a task most difficult and anxious in itself; the effort to get a fugitive treated with indulgence on his return. How delicate was the matter we may be reminded by an often-quoted parallel to St Paul's letter. His younger contemporary, the junior Pliny, a good example of the cultivated Roman gentleman, undertakes to plead with a friend, Sabinian, the cause of, not a slave but an ex-slave, a "freedman," who had offended. The stern law made it possible in such cases for the quondam master to claim the condemnation of the man back to slavery again.

Pliny addresses himself to the appeal with an unmistakable sense of difficulty and effort; he explains that he has spoken to the offender himself with the utmost severity; that to forgive him now will give Sabinian a strong position for very different conduct in the future, if necessary; that to put the youth to torture (it seems that Sabinian might have procured even this) would after all only inflict torture on his own kindly heart; and so on. The letter has its grace and beauty, and is evidently studied and elaborated to the utmost, for its difficult work. How shall the Cilician tent-maker do what the eminent and ennobled *littérateur* took such trouble over? He will do it with perfect ease, for he has what Pliny had not, the name of Jesus Christ to conjure with. He speaks indeed with a human tact and gentle dignity which leaves Pliny's behind, and which has won the admiration of non-Christian critics.[1] But his real strength and liberty in the work come evidently from the

---

[1] Renan calls the Epistle, "A true little masterpiece in the art of letter-writing"!

facts of grace and salvation. Paul, Philemon, and now equally Onesimus, are all *in the Lord*. Paul has found Christ, and is "His prisoner." Philemon has found Christ through Paul's ministry (ver. 19). Onesimus has found Christ. "Just as he was," disgraced, degraded, from the side of human law not a chattel only but a condemned victim, he has found the Lord, and the Lord has found him. Not all the Empire, not all society, can forbid him to be, as a penitent man who believes, "a member of Christ, the child of God, and an inheritor of the kingdom of heaven." Does Philemon own Christ for his absolute Master? Then, on his allegiance, he must recognize Onesimus as his spiritual brother in Him, antecedent to all other thoughts about him. With wonderful depth of holy tenderness this is put to him by St Paul (vers. 15, 16): "Perhaps he therefore was parted from thee for an hour, that thou mightest get him back for ever; no more as bondservant, but above bondservant, brother beloved, most of all to me, (yes, own brother to the Chosen Vessel,) but how much more (delightful logical inconsistency, for spiritual truth's sake) to thee, both in the flesh, and in the Lord?" The words seem to baffle not criticism only but praise; they take it for granted with the inimitable skill of love and holiness that Onesimus, in Christ, will be such to Philemon that his return will be infinitely welcome as a return *for ever*, a return to a companionship and fraternity that are never more to end.

It has been asked, did St Paul intend to press for Onesimus' emancipation? To me the question seems almost beneath the subject, as we read those two verses. That Philemon did legally manumit his slave is, to say the least of it, extremely probable. But surely if he did so it was on the principle that the less is included in the greater, and that the inconceivably greater was already granted to Onesimus from above—he was his master's brother in their Lord, now and for the eternal life. As such, he was close to his master's regenerate heart. He was welcomed back with a sacred domestic joy which echoed that which filled the house of the father of the

Prodigal, the father who would not hear the penitent out in his petition to be taken back as a servant.

How easy and how inimitable are the triumphs of grace, that is to say, of the Lord Jesus Christ by the Holy Ghost, over the most crooked and rugged problems of real human life! Its first and deepest conquest, necessary to all others, is over when the individual is brought face to face with his neglected or rejected Saviour, and finds himself falling at His feet, the willing captive of His love and power. But then the man, going out into life, spiritually stays still for ever in that blissful captivity; and it cannot but tell all around him in his attitude to other men. Everything is transfigured there for him. Personal grievances; invaded rights; all the rubs and frets of common hours, quite as much as the fierce temptations to pride and anger brought by some uncommon hours; these things now refuse to look the same to him as when he was "apart from Christ." He is no longer merely himself; he is "a man in Christ." And the offender either is in Christ too, or may be an hour hence; in any case, he is a fellow-sinner, and for him too Christ died.

All too feebly and intermittently, at the best, do we believers realize and apply these facts. But it is immensely important that we do *know* them for facts. And they have an actual influence in the world, even as things are, an influence which would be measured by a tremendous experienced difference if they should suddenly cease to be known.

Meantime, in studying the spiritual and social lessons of this precious "note," let us not forget Onesimus, and his point of view. We have stood at Philemon's side, and seen how for him the Lord Jesus would transfigure everything as He met Onesimus coming back again to that familiar door. But now, let us join Onesimus, and try to feel with him as he re-enters the old scene. For one thing, his being there at all is the token of a spiritual miracle. Without conversion, he would surely rather have put an end to his own life than returned of his free will all that way to Colossæ, a slave at law as much as ever.

But he has been converted. And with conversion, with the knowledge now of Christ for him and Christ in him, two profound effects have followed; he possesses a happiness which makes hard duties easy, and he has got a sight of holiness which makes duty divine. He returns to Philemon because, as God's providence suffered human society then to be, it was Philemon's right to have him; so not only does St Paul advise return, but Onesimus chooses it. And he returns to Philemon, we may be quite sure, as a brother in Christ indeed, but also, and for himself as the *first* thought, to be, in Christ, a willing, faithful, devoted bondservant, ready to take up every once repellent task (should it be ordered) not only without a murmur but with a happy heart, embracing the old position (should it be continued by his master's will) as no longer a degradation but now a great occasion for that most joyful of occupations, willing the will of God, delighting to do it, coveting *this* as the ambition of life, "that Christ may be magnified in my body."

Legend says that Onesimus became a bishop,

bishop of Ephesus. It is but legend; though undoubtedly many a primitive bishop, like Samuel Crowther in our own day, began life as a slave. But it matters very little to the noble significance of Onesimus' brief story whether or no he came to office in the Church. Even the episcopate is a much smaller thing in spiritual scale than the surrender of the soul in faith to God and to His will. And that great thing was given, most surely, by a sovereign hand, to the poor Phrygian slave.

So we watch him in at the courtyard door in the Colossian street. He enters with all modesty and humbleness of mien; not abject, not cringing, that is impossible now, in Christ; but penitent, submissive, ready. And there he is met with a glad chorus of Christian welcomes. Philemon first, and then Apphia, and Archippus, and surely their household too, are round him in a moment. "This *their brother* was dead, and is alive again; he was lost, and is found."

He presents the Letter. Its precise terms we are to study in our next chapter. But we know abundantly enough about it to make it precious to us already, as a message, an oracle indeed, full of the love of Christ, of the power of His grace upon the common things of life, and of the holiness of duty, that is to say, of conformity to the will of God.

# THE EPISTLE TO PHILEMON: TRANSLATION: "ENVOI"

Dieu a consolé son Fils sur la croix par la vue des enfans qu'il y engendroit : Jésus-Christ console ses ministres crucifiés avec luy, par la communication de la même grace.

>   Quesnel (1705), on Philem. 10.

Paul, handling a base and small matter, yet, according to his manner, mounteth aloft unto God.

>   The Geneva Bible (1557), heading to the Epistle.

We are all the Lord's Onesimi.

>   Luther.

# CHAPTER XIV

THE EPISTLE TO PHILEMON : TRANSLATION :
*ENVOI*

PHILEMON, while Onesimus stands once more before him, the new man in the old scene, reads as follows :

Ver. 1. **Paul, prisoner of Christ Jesus,** (he says nothing here of Apostleship; it is friend carrying to friend a common Master's message, and pointing as it were to the brand of suffering in that Master's service,) Paul, outwardly the captive of Roman law and power, but really of his Redeemer's will, **and Timotheus our (ὁ) brother** in the Lord's family, (for he too shall be named, and shall add his weight of sympathy and love,) **to Philemon**[1] **our beloved**

---

[1] "All we know of him is given in this short letter. . . . The Epistle indicates a noble specimen of the primitive Christian. . . . The name Philemon happens to occur in the beautiful legend of Philemon and Baucis, the *Phrygian*

Ver. 2. friend and fellow-worker, and to Apphia our (τῇ) sister,[1] and to Archippus our fellow-soldier[2] in the warfare of the Lord, and to the Church, the assembly of the converts, meeting at your house; using its chief room as the place of common worship.[3]

Ver. 3. **Grace to you, and peace, from God our Father, and from our Lord Jesus Christ.**[4]

Ver. 4. **I thank my God,** (characteristic words, for every Pauline letter except only Galatians opens

---

peasant pair, who, in an inhospitable neighbourhood, 'entertained unawares' Jupiter and Mercury (Ovid, *Metamorphoses*, viii. 626-724), 'gods in the likeness of men' (see Acts xiv. 11)." (Note here in *Camb. Bible for Schools, etc.*).—Philemon was the "fellow-worker" of the Apostle and his friends, no doubt, both by word and by general example and influence. We do not know whether he was set apart to special ministry. Legend makes him a bishop.

[1] Probably read ἀδελφῇ, not ἀγαπητῇ. "We may be sure that she was Philemon's wife. Her name was a frequent Phrygian name . . . and had no connexion with the Latin *Appia*." (Note here in *Cambridge Bible*.)

[2] This passage and Col. iv. 17 give us all we know about Archippus. The natural inference seems to be that he was son of Philemon and Apphia and mission-pastor at Colossæ; a ministry which in Epaphras' absence would have special responsibilities. Legend makes him a martyr with Philemon and Apphia.

[3] Perhaps Philemon's house was the one meeting-place in Colossæ, which was comparatively a small town.

[4] The salutation is verbatim as in Col. i. 2. See above, p. 25.

with thanksgiving; and it is St Paul only who uses in his letters that phrase of spiritual appropriation, "*my* God,"[1]) I thank Him, **always, when making mention of you,** naming the well-loved name and calling up its associations, **on occasion of** (ἐπί
Ver. 5. *c. gen.*) **my prayers**; **hearing,** as I have done, from Epaphras, and from your own Onesimus, **of your love and of your faith,** (your saving trust, root of all other blessings in your life,) **which you have**—the faith **towards** (πρός) **the Lord Jesus and the love unto** (εἰς) **all the saints,** that practical love which makes you the benefactor of every convert round you. And what is it that my thankful
Ver. 6. prayers seek for you? It is **that the fellowship of your faith,** the generous communication of your means, prompted by your personal salvation, **may prove effective,** all around you, **in producing a true knowledge** (ἐπίγνωσις) **of every good thing which is in us** (read, ἐν ἡμῖν), **unto Christ Jesus.** Yes, this is my dearest wish, my most earnest prayer; that your life of unselfish helpfulness may so tell around you that the observing world shall recognize, in your instance, all the beauty of the gifts Christ Jesus gives His people, so that praise shall come "unto Christ Jesus," aye, and new disciples too.

---

[1] In the New Testament we have it used elsewhere only by St Thomas (John xx. 28) and by the incarnate LORD Himself, Matt. xxvii. 46, etc., John xx. 17, Rev. ii. 7, iii. 12.

Ver. 7. **For much joy I had** (read χαράν and ἔσχον), when Epaphras gave me his report upon your life, and much encouragement to my own faith and zeal, on account of your love, thus shewn in its living fruits; for truly **the hearts** (σπλάγχνα) **of the saints,** the feelings of the poor and troubled converts around you, **have been rested,** refreshed and consoled, **through you, brother.** You have been the Lord's loving *agent* (διὰ σοῦ); He has used you as His almoner; well may I embrace you, in spirit, with a brother's arms.

Ver. 8. **Wherefore** now I approach you with a request, full of appeals to such faith and love. **Feeling** (ἔχων) though I do **large liberty** (παρρησίαν: lit., "liberty of speech," "outspokenness") **in Christ,** in our common union with Him, and so with one another, and recollecting that He used me to bring you into that union—liberty **to enjoin upon you,** with authority, **the befitting** action in the matter, yet

Ver. 9. **on account of the love** between us, (and of the love which shines in your life,) I rather **appeal to** (παρακαλῶ) **you. For I am just**[1] **Paul, aged**[2] **Paul,**

---

[1] I attempt thus to paraphrase the exquisite phrase, τοιοῦτος ὤν ὡς, κ.τ.λ.

[2] Πρεσβύτης. So all manuscripts; and this is confirmed by the ancient Versions (e.g. *Paulus senex*, Latin). Lightfoot advocates the reading πρεσβευτής, "an ambassador"; comparing Eph. vi. 20, πρεσβεύω ἐν ἁλύσει, "I am *on embassy*

aye, and prisoner of Christ Jesus now. What is my
Ver. 10. petition then? I appeal to you about my
own child,¹ whom I begot,² to the new life, in my
Ver. 11. (τοῖς: omit μου) bonds, Onesimus.³ You
once found him (τόν ποτέ σοι) profitless (in sorrowful
contrast to his *name*!), but you will find him—and
Ver. 12. so shall I—right profitable now.⁴ Him (ὅν)

---

in chains," and remarking that the Greeks often spelt πρεσ-
βεύτης without its second ε. But may we not say that an
allusion to the writer's sacred *dignity* is not quite in place
here, just after he has expressly declined to speak with
authority, and just when he is dealing with the *pathos* of
his position? The very phrase τοιοῦτος ὢν οἷος is of a kind
which much better introduces an argument from weakness
than from prerogative.—St Paul was probably about sixty
years old when he wrote; quite old enough, *in such a life*,
to justify a reference to age.

¹ Περὶ τοῦ ἐμοῦ τέκνου. The phrase is just a little stronger
than π. τοῦ τέκνου μου, and I have attempted, with hesitation,
to convey this by the insertion of "own."

² He puts the conversion quite into the past, by this aorist;
for it would be long past when Philemon read these words.

³ "The name stands last in the sentence . . . a perfect
touch of heart-rhetoric." (Note here in the *Cambridge Bible*.)
It was a common slave-name, and meant *Helpful, Useful*.
Such laudatory names for the class were usual; e.g. *Chrestus*,
"Good," *Symphorus*, "Advantageous."

⁴ I have freely paraphrased the Greek here.—Lightfoot
remarks that καὶ ἐμοί is "an after-thought . . . According
to common Greek usage the first person would . . . precede
the second."

I send back[1] to you (read σοι), him (αὐτόν), that is to say, mine own heart,[2] my vitals (σπλάγχνα); an object of the tenderest affection in the Lord, one with me in the mighty link of the spiritual birth.

Ver. 13. **Him** (ὅν) **I, personally,** (the ἐγώ is emphatic,) **was wishing** (but duty crossed the wish) **to keep fast** (κατέχειν) at my own side, so that—**on your behalf** (ὑπὲρ σοῦ), as your substitute, your representative—**he might serve me,** in personal attendance, **in the bonds of the Gospel,** in this imprisonment for the Lord's work's sake; *Onesimus* might indeed have been *helpful* under such conditions!

Ver. 14. **But apart from your decision I declined to do anything, that your goodness**—in giving him over to me, had that been possible—**might not have the look of compulsion** (ὡς κατ' ἀνάγκην), **but be all of free-will.**[3]

---

[1] Lit., "I did send." The aorist is "epistolary," written from the *recipient's* point of view.—Let us note as we pass on that this brief word must conceal behind it a great sacrifice on St Paul's part, a sacrifice of deep heart-affection (and of much practical convenience) to the demands of duty. Onesimus' own obedience to "I ought" was scarcely greater.

[2] The Received Text reads, ὃν ἀνέπεμψα· σὺ δὲ αὐτόν, τουτέστι τὰ ἐμὰ σπλάγχνα, προσλαβοῦ. But there is good evidence for the reading, ὃν ἀνέπεμψά σοι, αὐτόν, τουτέστι τὰ ἐμὰ σπλάγχνα, omitting προσλαβοῦ.

[3] "It might seem that he almost suggests to Philemon to *send Onesimus back to him*. But this is not likely in itself, in view of the long and costly journey involved; and besides,

So he returns, as an act of duty, on his part and on mine. But is it not also because of a benignant
Ver. 15. purpose of the Lord's? **For perhaps it was for this**, for this occasion of return, of *such* return, **that he was severed from you for a season** (πρὸς ὥραν); **that you might get him back**[1] **for ever** (αἰώνιον), an *eternal* recovery, for earth and then for heaven. And now you get him back, a possession more precious far than when he went;
Ver. 16. **no more as bondservant,** (for, whatever you do or do not do with his legal relation to you, that now sinks into something greater,) **but more than bondservant, even brother beloved, most of all to me,** (for "my child Onesimus" is my brother too, in the family of God,) **but how much more**—for my "most of all" must yield to yours—**to you,** joined to you as he now is **alike in the flesh,**[2] **and in the Lord**;

---

he looks forward to visit Colossæ himself before long (ver. 22). What he means is that he sends back Onesimus, because to retain him would be to get a benefit from Philemon willing *or not*, and Philemon's 'good' had always been freely given." (Note here in the *Cambridge Bible*.)

[1] Ἀπέχῃς. The "verb is often used of *receiving payment*; e.g. Matt. vi. 2, 5, 16. We might almost paraphrase, '*get him paid back*,' as if he had been '*lent to the Lord.*'" (Note in the *Cambridge Bible*.)

[2] "A remarkable phrase, as if slavery were a sort of relationship. This thought appears, as a fact, in combination (and contrast) with the harshest theories of ancient slavery. Thus Aristotle (*Polity* i. ii. . . .) writes, 'the slave is *a portion*

as it were your limb, your hand, in earthly service, and your fellow-limb in the Redeemer's body!

Ver. 17. **If you hold me then as your partner in faith and life, welcome him as me**; it is my other self who comes to you.

Ver. 18. **But you may have other charges against him**, besides his flight. **If he wronged you, defrauded you**, taking what was yours when he fled, **or if he owes you anything**, having had money entrusted to him for use, and having let it go, **put that down to**

Ver. 19. **me; I Paul write it** (ἔγραψα, epistolary) **with my own hand; I will myself refund it.** My autograph is here, to secure your claim; my amanuensis gives way here to *my* pen, that I may give you legal bond; **not to say to you, however, that you actually** (καί) **owe me your own self besides.** Besides the gain, through me, of getting Onesimus back *a new man*, you have got through me the gain of your own salvation, your self made new in Christ.

Ver. 20. **Yes, brother, let me, even me,**[1] **have joy** (ὀναίμην) **of you**, win glad benefit from you, **in the Lord**[2]; **rest my heart** (σπλάγχνα) **in Christ** (read,

---

of his master; as it were a living though separated portion of *his body*.' The Gospel would of course 'enforce with all its power *that* aspect of the connexion.'" (Note in the *Cambridge Bible*.)

[1] Ἐγώ is emphatic.
[2] Surely ὀναίμην is a gracious play upon the name Ὀνήσιμος:

Ver. 21. ἐν Χριστῷ). **Relying on your obedience, the obedience of affection to affection, I write (ἔγραψα) to you, knowing that you will do even beyond what (ἅ) I say.**

Ver. 22. **And (δέ) meanwhile, to mention another matter, distinct, yet not without its connexion, please also to prepare me hospitality in Colossæ; for I hope that, by means of your prayers, offered as I know they have been for my release, I shall be granted to you, as a gift from the hand of God to those who love me well.**

Ver. 23. **There greet you Epaphras, my fellow-prisoner-**
Ver. 24. **of-war in Christ Jesus; Marcus, Aristarchus, Demas, Lucas, my fellow-workers.**[1]

Ver. 25. **The grace of our Lord Jesus Christ be with your (ὑμῶν) spirit. Amen.** Even so; let that "grace" which is in fact Himself in His present power for blessing be with "the spirit" of you all, the one true inner life of your whole circle. Amen.

It is indeed a wonderful letter. If my reader's heart goes at all with mine, he agrees with me that it is indeed a *Scripture*, not

---

almost as if he would say, let me get help as well as you get Helpful.

[1] See above, pp. 263, 264, for these names at the close of the Epistle to the Colossians.

only by the solemn attestation of the Christian Church, but on the inner evidence of its mysterious depth and richness. Short as it is, I never for my own part read the Epistle to Philemon without a fresh sense that it shares that peculiar characteristic of the Bible at large—you never get to the end, to the depth.

Among other living lessons, one or two have, during this "study," touched me particularly.

i. I am awestruck by the testimony of the Letter to the sanctity of duty. Was this ever more nobly illustrated than in these unobtrusive lines? Onesimus has found the Lord, in full salvation, probably after awful experiences of the miseries of transgression; and he has found, incidentally, a father and a brother at once in Paul. Paul has found Onesimus, as that singularly delightful and rich discovery, a human soul whom the finder has been permitted to win for Jesus Christ. The Phrygian slave has become his "son," his "heart," his other self; indescribably dear to him, with an affection in which the strong element of compassion blends with all the rest, natural and spiritual. Was there ever a tie of the kind which pleaded more winningly to be kept if possible intact? And was it not easy to manage the circumstances so that it should not be disturbed? But no; in the glow of Christian love the glory of Christian law stands out only the brighter. What was right? It was right that Onesimus should unconditionally go back. It was right that St Paul should let him, should bid him, go without reserve. It must be so, as a duty in the abstract. It must be so yet more as a duty in the glorious concrete; it concerned the Lord Jesus Christ; it touched His honour; it was necessary—if He was to be fully understood as the Lord at once and equally of love and of truth.

"Dig in the Bible where you will, only dig deep enough, and you will find *Do right* at the bottom." We have not to dig very deep for this in the Letter to Philemon.

ii. On the other hand, the Epistle is a perfect example of the *manner* of the Gospel in its inculcation of duty. It is absolutely decided, yet how entirely gentle! Here is no " Stoic rigour," still less any Pharisaic hardness (though the writer was a Pharisee), calling attention to itself. The thing is done, and done thoroughly. But it is done as by one who enters deep into every feeling of every one concerned. He perfectly understands Onesimus, and while he treats him as just what he is, he speaks of him in the very way to shield him and to secure his kindly welcome back. He understands Philemon equally well, and takes account with a fine insight and respect of all his grievance and his claim. And he knows his own heart too, in its sensibilities of attachment, and makes not the least affectation of having crushed them or frozen them in the business of doing right.

All this is just in the manner of the Gospel. No such power has ever appeared on earth to the rescue of Duty, as the Gospel. But it comes to the rescue with an energy which is wholly of sacred love. It is the glorifier of Right, but so that it is always also the friend of the human heart.

iii. Lastly, as the Christian reads this brief radiant page, he is conscious all along that it is, besides all else that it is, a parable—of himself. "We are all the Lord's Onesimi," wrote blessed Luther. Is it not so? Let the sinner who has been convinced by the Spirit, brought to believing repentance, and received by the Lord who brought him, answer the question.

He was always, by every right and claim which could give possession, the property, the personal chattel, of Jesus Christ. But till grace regenerated his will, he was a restive servant, a rebel, a fugitive, a defrauder and debtor to that Master. He traversed strange and distant paths in his guilty flight. Whatever they were in outward seeming, they were all "ways of the transgressor" in their inwardness. The unconverted life may have been scandalous, or it may have been singularly seemly. But as regarded the true claims of the true Master, the wanderer's deep being was saying through it all, "I will not have this Man to reign over me."

Then came, somehow or other, "the time

of finding." The fugitive, by whatever means, "came to himself," and discovered first his misery and then his wonderful redemption from it, through One who had borne his burthen, and who lived to be his life. And lo, in this case, for here the parable breaks down under its divine antitype, his Paul and his Philemon are one; the Friend who finds him in his wretchedness proves to be the Master whom he has rejected in his miserable pride.

So this Onesimus awakens to the stern but most blessed duty of a prompt return and an unconditional surrender to the bondage of the Lord. He cannot rest now away from his Colossæ. He will never find happiness now, this he knows perfectly well, except within the gate of his Philemon's house. He makes haste to the place which he had once, in the Fall, mistaken for a prison, but which he knows now as the place where he is possessed, that he may posess all things in his MASTER.

He comes back, without a word of self-defence, to give himself up. He places his Lord's foot upon his neck. He takes up every condition of his Lord's discipline, "to love, to cherish, to obey." He lays his Lord's burthen on his shoulder, rejoicing. He comes for his Lord's orders; and the one ambition of his life is now to do them.

He is perfectly free, for he has seen the interior of the bondservice of Jesus Christ, and assents from his own soul's depths to the bliss of belonging to Him.

Never can he forget the wrong and shame of his spiritual treachery and escapade. Well does he know that had his Philemon *taken the law* with him his just lot would have been "many stripes," and "shame and everlasting contempt." He never forgives himself, remembering his sin and knowing, now at last, his Lord.

But all this means no misgiving. He is more than ever his Lord's bondman; yes, the bondman who has now said with all his heart, "I will not go out free," as it were countersigning irrevocably the document of his own purchase. But he is most of all his Lord's brother; wonderful word. His Philemon "is not ashamed to call" him so with his own lips. He is "received back for ever, brother beloved." Yet again, the brother is always and for ever the bondservant; for his whole existence is surrounded and indelibly charactered by the fact that he belongs. Only, it is a belonging full of life as well as of law. He is "a portion of his Master; as it were a living, though separated, portion of His body."[1]

"I serve" is henceforth a fact absolutely necessary to the expression of his affinity, and of his love. It is so now, it will be so for ever, when the Colossæ of his earthly sojourn with the Lord is transfigured into "that great City, the holy Jerusalem." For there also it is written (Rev. xxii. 3) that " His bondservants shall do Him service."

The glorified shall be still "the Onesimi" of the Lord:

QUEM NOSSE VIVERE, CUI SERVIRE REGNARE EST.
AMEN.

---

[1] See above, p. 309.